The Entrepreneur's Field Guide

The 3 Day Startup Method

New Teaching Resources for Management in a Globalised World

Print ISSN: 2661-4774
Online ISSN: 2661 4782

Series Editor: Professor Léo-Paul Dana

The classic economic view of internationalisation was based on the theory of competitive advantage, and over the years, internationalisation was seen in various lights, as an expansion option. With the reduction of trade barriers, however, many local small enterprises face major international competitors in formerly protected domestic markets. Today, competitiveness in the global marketplace is no longer an option; it has become a necessity as the acceleration towards globalisation offers unprecedented challenges and opportunities.

This book series will bring together textbooks, monographs, edited collections and handbooks useful to postgraduates and researchers in the age of globalisation. Relevant topics include, but are not limited to: research methods, culture, entrepreneurship, globalisation, immigration, migrants, public policy, self-employment, sustainability, technological advances, emerging markets, demographic shifts, and innovation.

Published:

New Teaching
Resources for
Management in a
Globalised World
Volume 3

The Entrepreneur's Field Guide

The 3 Day Startup Method

Andrew Zimbroff
University of Nebraska-Lincoln, USA

Cam Houser
University of Texas at Austin

 **World Scientific**

NEW JERSEY · LONDON · SINGAPORE · BEIJING · SHANGHAI · HONG KONG · TAIPEI · CHENNAI · TOKYO

Published by

World Scientific Publishing Co. Pte. Ltd.

5 Toh Tuck Link, Singapore 596224

USA office: 27 Warren Street, Suite 401-402, Hackensack, NJ 07601

UK office: 57 Shelton Street, Covent Garden, London WC2H 9HE

Library of Congress Cataloging-in-Publication Data
Names: Zimbroff, Andrew, author. | Houser, Cam, author.
Title: The entrepreneur's field guide : the 3 day startup method /
    Andrew Zimbroff, University of Nebraska-Lincoln, USA, Cam Houser.
Description: Hackensack, NJ : World Scientific, 2022. | Series: New teaching resources
    for management in a globalised world, 2661-4774 ; 3 |
    Includes bibliographical references and index.
Identifiers: LCCN 2021030577 | ISBN 9789811236693 (hardcover) |
    ISBN 9789811236709 (ebook) | ISBN 9789811236716 (ebook other)
Subjects: LCSH: New business enterprises--Handbooks, manuals, etc. |
    Entrepreneurship--Handbooks, manuals, etc.
Classification: LCC HD62.5 .Z56 2022 | DDC 658.1/1--dc23
LC record available at https://lccn.loc.gov/2021030577

British Library Cataloguing-in-Publication Data
A catalogue record for this book is available from the British Library.

For any available supplementary material, please visit
https://www.worldscientific.com/worldscibooks/10.1142/12269#t=suppl

Desk Editor: Ong Shi Min Nicole

Typeset by Stallion Press
Email: enquiries@stallionpress.com

Printed in Singapore

Acknowledgments

The authors would like to acknowledge the following individuals for their contributions to 3 Day Startup:

Joel Hestness, Thomas Finsterbush, Ruchit Shah, Bart Bohn, Jeremy Guillory, Vikram Deverajan, Vanessa Castaneda, Cristal Glanchai, Pat Condon, Jason Seats, Graham Weston, Lorenzo Gomez, Josh Baer, Dr. Steve Nichols, Isaac Barchas, Lou Agnese, Paul Hurdlow, Michael Akillian, Madeline Vu, Maia Donohue, Christoph Zahn, Max Ulm, Ash Maurya, Bob Metcalfe, Ross Burhdorf.

And the hundreds of organizers, volunteers, and participants who took part in the programs along the journey — you are all the most important figures in this entire process and we couldn't have done it without you.

Contents

Foreword

The History of the 3 Day Startup organization

3 Day Startup (3DS) did not become the global non-profit it is today overnight, and both of the authors have enjoyed watching the organization grow into what it is today. Further, this history has largely influenced what the organization is today, and why we approach entrepreneurship education in the way that we do.

In 2008, a small group of graduate students at The University of Texas at Austin (UT Austin) lamented that there were extremely limited entrepreneurship education opportunities available. Entrepreneurship wasn't nearly as prominent or popular as it is today, and universities did not prioritize it as a career path for their students upon graduation. Further, the entrepreneurship education that was available wasn't very good — it was often limited primarily to business students, and it treated startups like small versions of Fortune 500 companies (they are very different, and different skills are required for large, established entities vs. turning a business concept into a scalable, profitable business while managing volatility and highly scarce resources). Further, when available, this education often relied on simulations and case studies, which we now know are not the best ways to teach skills important to entrepreneurship.

The problem described above was experienced by many different students at UT Austin. Subsequently, these students that comprised the early founders of 3DS (Joel Hestness, Thomas

Finsterbusch, Cameron Houser, Ruchit Shah, and Jeremy Guillory) represented multiple disciplines of study: they came from the Colleges of Business, Law, Engineering, with early participants coming from additional departments of the university. While not planned at the time, this led to a core philosophy of the organization: that entrepreneurship is for everyone, and should not be "owned" by any particular field. Further, by having program participants from multiple backgrounds, it created an opportunity for students to work in multidisciplinary teams, an experience that is important for many career paths (not just entrepreneurship), but not available to many students confined by a single academic major.

Due to the student-driven nature of the initial organization, 3DS initially focused on informal learning environments (i.e. those that take place outside of classes that lead to college credit). Further, this meant that those we were trying to reach had other commitments, leaving them with limited time for entrepreneurial pursuits. This led us to initially focus on programming that would begin on Friday afternoon and end on Sunday evening. Our assumption was that almost anyone can dedicate a weekend to trying out entrepreneurship, even those with limited time. This proved to be correct, and to this day a majority of programs that the 3 Day Startup organization delivers are this length, and frequently occur on weekends.

The first 3DS programs

The initial 3DS programs could be described as "controlled chaos." We had a basic overall structure and timeline for the educational programs. However, we placed participants "in the driver's seat" to control their own learning experience. They pitched startup ideas to work on, and voted on their favorite ones. They also formed their own teams with which they worked for a majority of the program. As a result, every 3DS program has its own unique flavor, shaped largely by its participants.

We knew early on that a primary element of the programs should be experiential learning, or "learning by doing." We decided to "kick participants out of the building" in order to actually go speak with real potential customers. This remains a core component of all 3DS programs to this day, and we continue to place a large emphasis on customer engagement (an entire chapter of the book is dedicated to this as well).

While we were initially unsure how this untested program format would be received, the feedback was highly encouraging. Program participants were highly enthusiastic and engaged during the program. This enthusiasm led to them trying to get as much done as possible, as well as come up with some innovative ways that participants could work to develop their business concepts. For example, some teams would call Hawaii on Friday evening, using time zones to reach potential customers during business hours. Many participants would also stay up extremely late (and sometimes all night) to get as much done as possible during a program. When we would give out informal awards (to highlight noteworthy actions like a unique approach to customer discovery), the "trophy" was a can of Red Bull spray-painted gold, recognizing the hard work and late nights our participants would contribute.

Expansion

After running a few programs, it seemed like there was a recurring interest and support for 3DS as an extracurricular at UT Austin. There were further indicators that there was an opportunity for impactful programs beyond a single post-secondary institution. 3DS alumni, highly enthusiastic after program participation, told their friends, both at UT and other schools, about the experience. Soon, we received inquiries about hosting 3DS workshops at other institutions. Some of the first places we expanded to were other schools in Texas like Trinity University and Texas A&M University. A German foreign exchange student at UT brought a 3DS workshop to RWTH Aachen University, which to this day regularly holds 3DS workshops.

Challenges arose for how to scale this idea beyond Austin. If this was an organization that would grow, it would need people dedicated to organizing programs. Fortunately, the Central Texas entrepreneurship community came to our aid. Donors like Pat Condon offered early financial support to lay the basic groundwork for the 3 Day Startup organization as a nonprofit. Austin Technology Incubator helped provide in-kind support, in the form of office space, venues to host our workshops, and advice based on their extensive experience in the Austin startup ecosystem. This help was crucial to the establishment of the 3 Day Startup organization, the 501(c)3 nonprofit which came to replace the UT Austin Student organization.

How to achieve financial sustainability was another question we had to answer as an organization. We decided to pursue earned revenue as the main source of funding for the organization. This was done based on the belief that it was more consistent than relying on donors and highly variable grant cycles. It would allow us to spend less time fundraising, and more time implementing entrepreneurship programs. Further, it allowed us to "practice what we preached" — providing something of value to paying customers. This decision also ensured that we were in tune with what our customers wanted. Even to this day, while the organization's customers have changed, we remain focused on ensuring our curriculum remains up to date and relevant for those we serve.

New landscapes, customers, and challenges

A few years after its inception, the 3 Day Startup organization was an established organization. It was running multiple programs annually at universities around the US (and some other countries). It had full-time employees to scale the organization. However, we were facing a different landscape than when the organization was initially founded. People were becoming more aware of the importance of entrepreneurship, and more people were interested in entrepreneurial careers. Universities were recognizing it as a viable career option, and allocating real resources to entrepreneurship centers and coursework. Further, educators were starting to learn that experiential learning was the most effective way to train aspiring entrepreneurs. Overall, this was a great thing — it meant more opportunities for empowering aspiring entrepreneurs. However, it meant that our customers had more options for entrepreneurship education. The organization would have to evolve to remain relevant in an environment with more entrepreneurship education opportunities.

We started to explore implementing educational programs for customers outside of post-secondary institutions. One first area of expansion was established companies that admired startups' ability for innovation, creativity, and rapid execution and pivoting. However, these companies (including "grown up" startups) had difficulty recreating this culture in-house. We found that 3DS programs could be a tool to help spur innovation internally. This led to the creation of 3DS Enterprise programs, first held within corporate headquarters of Austin-based companies like HomeAway and RetailMeNot. To this day, these programs remain a core offering of the organization.

We also expanded our international programs beyond that which we already delivered at international post-secondary institutions. We trained facilitators in multiple countries so that we could deliver programs more frequently and effectively. We also began to host exchange programs, where international visitors came to the US to experience its entrepreneurial culture. One example of such programs is the recurring Austria to Austin program, which brings Austrian nationals to Austin for an exchange program focused on entrepreneurship development. 3DS is now a truly global organization thanks to these ongoing efforts and programs.

Part of the magic of 3DS is the amazing participants that we meet during all of our educational programs. However, alumni don't often get the opportunity to meet others in the 3DS family outside of their program. We began hosting an annual conference in Austin called Global Roundup. This allowed alumni from all over the world to gather in a single place, and interact with others that had gone through the same entrepreneurial journey. Further, the conference continued the focus on practices important for entrepreneurs, with extensive real-world applicability. It was an amazing feeling seeing 3DS family members from half a dozen countries interacting with each other over breakfast tacos (an Austin delicacy, which we make sure to have at every Global Roundup). Further, it allows us to continue interactions with our alumni and organizers after program completion.

Today, we are proud of the 3DS's growth from its humble origins, all that it has accomplished, and what the organization is today. However, we know that we will not remain static for long. Like startups, the landscape of entrepreneurship education is changing, and 3DS will have to adapt to these changes as well. Still, we remain optimistic of what the organization can accomplish.

The Impact of 3DS on an Entrepreneurship Ecosystem: A Case Study

Malshini Senaratne is the Director of Eco Sol Consulting in the Seychelles. She has been an organizer and researcher with the organization since 2018.

Dr. Andrew Zimbroff and I were never destined to meet. This is partially explained by the fact that I live and work in the Seychelles, a group of 115 low lying islands scattered across the Indian Ocean, while he resides in the United States. Therefore, some background might be necessary in explaining how Andrew and I are presently collaborating on our third grant in the Seychelles, where we are working on improving the islands' entrepreneurship ecosystem and helping aspiring entrepreneurs in achieving their dreams.

In 2017, I was selected along with 999 other participants across the African continent to take part in the Young African Leaders Initiative flagship program, the Mandela Washington Fellowship. This Fellowship allowed African leaders in the spheres of civil society, entrepreneurship, and public engagement to take part in summer programs in selected American universities across the States. You would think this explains how Andrew and I met, but I was placed at Rutgers University, New Jersey, and he was based at the University of Nebraska–Lincoln! Fortunately, 3DS was a global startup spanning large geographic distances to connect the Seychelles, Texas, and Nebraska.

Upon completion of this Fellowship, various grants became available to Fellows to pursue their interests in their home countries with the help of American professionals. 3DS immediately caught my eye; the non-governmental organization had already taken part in the Exchange program and had stellar reputation due to the success of their program in Malawi. I was very impressed by the stories that emanated from the Malawi experience and wished to replicate this success in the Seychelles. Entrepreneurship has been encouraged by the Seychelles government in recent years as a way of diversifying the economic base and alleviating poverty. However, the ecosystem had fundamental gaps that suggested startup ideation would generate much needed innovation and creativity.

As the Director of Research at 3DS at the time, I did not expect Andrew to travel all the way to the Seychelles to facilitate a 3DS program (though, let's face it, I assume no one would turn down going to the beautiful tropical islands of the Seychelles). However, due to various eligibility and scheduling requirements, he ended up being the facilitator assigned to this program. Under Andrew's guidance, 3DS turned out to be the perfect vehicle to provide a much-needed boost to the entrepreneurial culture in my country. 3DS's approach to entrepreneurial startup training is different from any other experience provided. I've had the pleasure of witnessing 3 such programs in the Seychelles since 3DS partnered with my company Eco Sol Consulting, and I never get tired of seeing the participants' excitement and delight at the end of a successful program.

What makes 3DS different? Their approach is participant-centric; the onus is on the entrepreneur to put in the hard work and reap the rewards. In this way, 3DS inculcates budding entrepreneurs with a key life lesson; reap what you sow. Furthermore, the training is not classroom based. The company believes in iterative learning, or learning by doing. By literally "kicking the class out into the market," 3DS ensures participants get on-the-ground exposure to product ideation, collaboration, design, research, and refinement of the business idea. This approach has pushed the chances of a new venture's success to even better heights.

Andrew and I have implemented three such programs in the Seychelles, all of them accomplishing various forms of success. The satisfaction I have drawn is from seeing actual, viable ventures spring up as a result of this training. In our own way, we have influenced the lives of entrepreneurs in Seychelles, which is something that I am proud of. We have enjoyed working together ever since we embarked on that first program back in 2018, and we hope to maintain that collaboration. We were successful in securing a grant in 2019 to assess the baseline Blue Economy entrepreneurship ecosystem in the Seychelles.

Since then, 3DS's influence has taken on national importance in the Seychelles. Eco Sol Consulting once again partnered with Andrew to provide national-level training and capacity development strategies around entrepreneurship in collaboration with the Seychelles Enterprise Agency, a government body assisting Small- to Medium-sized businesses on the island. Through this partnership, the government hopes to enhance their service offering to entrepreneurs in the country and truly expand the potential of new venture creation.

3DS's impact on the Seychelles cannot be minimized. Every training program the organization facilitated in this country has seen the creation of at least five new ventures or the registration of new venture ideas by its participants. These startups join the ranks of the more than 150 startups launched by 3DS alumni. The community created by 3DS here goes beyond the confines of the classroom as well. Even beyond our borders, its powerful global network brings together aspiring and inspirational entrepreneurs from across the globe and serves to push true innovation forward. With a presence in 35 countries across six continents, the company's impact on the global entrepreneurial ecosystem cannot be denied.

To me, however, 3DS means so much more. The interaction with stellar trainers such as Andrew has raised the bar for entrepreneurial development in the country. The 3DS family on the island has stayed strong, with regular meet ups and continued collaboration on the ideas that were generated during a three-day workshop. Through Andrew and the 3DS family, Seychellois entrepreneurs have realized that on these islands too, their entrepreneurial dreams matter.

The funny thing is, Dr. Andrew Zimbroff and I were never even destined to meet.

Note from the Authors (How to Use This Book)

This book adopts a similar philosophy to that which is applied to 3DS educational programs. It places a strong emphasis on "learning by doing." As a result, you won't encounter much high-level theory or academic principles within. Instead, this work focuses much more on introducing and guiding you through actions that actually take place during startup creation. By completing these actions, you will learn skills important for all early-stage entrepreneurs. Further, by applying these actions to a business concept of your choosing, you will better understand how to apply them to business creation, and potentially lay the groundwork for a real business in the future.

This book also includes many real-world examples from entrepreneurs we have worked with. These examples further show how to apply the skills introduced in this work. In the more than 10 years that we have been teaching 3DS educational programs, we have constantly been refining and improving the curriculum that we deliver to make it as effective as possible. However, the emphasis on pragmatic, actionable teaching has remained constant, and we are confident it is one of the best ways to learn entrepreneurial skills.

It has been amazing to watch 3DS grow from a small student organization at The University of Texas at Austin to a global non-profit reaching thousands of alumni in dozens of countries. One key to this successful growth has been adaptability and willingness to accommodate new challenges as we delivered workshops in new settings. This adaptability was also one of the motivating forces for this book. As much as we would want to, we cannot go everywhere and train everyone. This book allows us to reach aspiring entrepreneurs that we otherwise couldn't with educational programming alone, expanding the reach and impact of our educational efforts.

While there are common principles for all entrepreneurs world-wide, we also must be aware of local conditions. The challenges that Blue Economy entrepreneurs in the Seychelles face can be vastly different from Austrian Tech entrepreneurs (both of these groups have been trained by the 3 Day Startup organization). While the content of this book is applicable in a wide range of entrepreneurial settings, there is still the need to tailor its application for specific settings. This is where you come in.

We hope you enjoy this book, and that it becomes a useful tool on your entrepreneurial journey.

Andrew Zimbroff and Cameron Houser

Part 1
Is Entrepreneurship for You?

Chapter 1

Is Entrepreneurship for You?

1.1 The Benefits of Entrepreneurship as a Career

There are multiple elements of an entrepreneurial career that are appealing and help draw people to this career path. Many enjoy the exciting and fast-paced work environment encountered at startups. These businesses often have rapid expansion, which can lead to changing roles and focuses. What you work on can change dramatically over the course of months (or even weeks). Working for a startup is rarely boring (something which can't be said for many other jobs).

Further, there is potential for rapid upward mobility when working in a startup. These businesses are growing quickly, and as an employee of these ventures, you are coming along for the ride (while helping propel the ride at the same time). As a business grows, your current position will gain responsibilities and importance. This upward mobility is much faster than in a more traditional business role — no waiting for your supervisor to retire, or for that dream job to open up at another company — your position will grow, sometimes without even planning for it. As a result, many ambitious people are drawn to startups as a way to accelerate career mobility.

Most startup work environments are very non-rigid — they are open to most work configurations, as long as you are able to successfully complete all responsibilities for your position. If you don't like wearing a suit and tie to work every day, or starting work at 8:00 am sharp, most startups allow for flexibility on a day-to-day basis. Further, there are few entrenched processes and attitudes, and most new ventures are open to new ideas if they lead to an improvement over the current practices. For many, this laid back atmosphere allows people to be comfortable, minimizing stress and maximizing their productivity.

Finally, if the business succeeds, you can make a lot of money (though this is unlikely from a purely statistical standpoint). This doesn't just apply to the founders. Most early employees receive some form of ownership in the company (referred to as "equity"). This sense of ownership creates benefits beyond the potential financial reward of equity — your coworkers are much more likely to be motivated and passionate for the success of your business. This passionate and enthusiastic environment can be an inspiring and motivating force for many, and drives many to entrepreneurial career paths.

A combination of some or all of the reasons above make entrepreneurial careers appealing (though you might have already known some or all of that).

1.2 Before We Continue, Let's Try to Talk You Out of This

Entrepreneurship is not all positive — like any job, there are pros and there are cons. It would be a disservice to you to withhold the negative aspects of entrepreneurial careers, or to push you towards a career path using incomplete information.

When we say "talk you out of this," we are not trying to discourage you (or anyone else) from a career path you are interested in — As we've stated repeatedly, we want to have as many innovators as possible. We are merely trying to give an objective perspective that portrays both positive and negative realities of entrepreneurship. It is up to you to determine if the positive elements outweigh the negative ones, and if entrepreneurship is a good fit for you. The best way this book can help you with that is by presenting comprehensive information in an objective manner, and letting you decide for yourself.

There is no single set of qualities necessary for entrepreneurs to be successful. However, past research has identified some ethos and attitudes frequently found within successful entrepreneurs. In this chapter, we are going to introduce some of these findings, and help you better determine if you possess some of the traits important for entrepreneurial careers. Further, if entrepreneurship is not a good fit for you, that's ok — it doesn't make you a failure in any way, and there are tons of non-entrepreneurial careers that are meaningful and impactful. If this is the case, you want to figure this out as soon as possible (it's like being Lean, but for yourself), so that you can instead invest your time and focus on a career path that is a better match.

In this chapter, we will introduce some questions based on common occurrences within entrepreneurship, as well as possible responses to these scenarios. There is no single correct answer to these questions (it's not a bubble test, we promise), and the answers do not even represent all possible responses. However, they do represent some patterns observed by the authors and many others within startup environments. We also call on academic research that

---

Dispelling Common Entrepreneurship Myths

In the last few years, entrepreneurship has seemingly become more popular. As a result of this trend, startups have had increasing appearances in the mainstream media (TV shows like Silicon Valley and Shark Tank come to mind). This is a great thing — we want to see many people innovating and creating ventures that generate jobs and economic development — and pop culture can be a positive force in encouraging this. However, sometimes pop culture and others don't always portray entrepreneurship accurately, leading to some misconceptions. In an attempt to correct some of this misinformation, the following are some of the more common misconceptions about entrepreneurship, as well as a more accurate description of similar themes.

(*Continued*)

(Continued)

Myth #1: Entrepreneurship is easy

While entrepreneurship can be highly enjoyable and fulfilling, it is almost always more challenging than other career paths. You are attempting to create a financially sustainable startup from the ground up. There is usually no precedent or example for how to approach many of the tasks you need to accomplish. Further, you are doing all of this with limited resources and time, and there is little room for error. As a result of this difficulty, as many as 80% of new businesses fail or are unprofitable. While many entrepreneurs find this challenge highly enjoyable and motivating, there are usually less difficult career approaches.

In a similar vein, people sometimes assume that because most startup work environments are casual, the work is not that difficult. It's true that many startup employees don't have to be in the office exactly at 8:00 am, and come to work in jeans and t-shirts. However, that doesn't mean you're not working long hours with limited resources and support. A casual and egalitarian work environment is liberating for many people, and is what drives them to endure the more challenging aspects of entrepreneurship. But casual does not mean easy, and the two are not the same thing.

Myth #2: Entrepreneurs possess all knowledge that they need before they start their business

Entrepreneurship entails creating a business from the ground up, where all aspects of the business didn't exist before you started. As a result, there will be many times of uncertainty and dealing with challenges you haven't encountered previously. There is no single major skill or a set of skills that will cover all elements of starting a business. There are ways to mitigate these challenges — you can learn some of the more frequently occurring skills (many of which we introduce in this book). Alternatively, you can rely on your professional network for help, or quickly learn new skills as needed (you won't become an expert, but you can often do things "good enough.")

Sometimes we get asked, "What is the best major or educational background for entrepreneurship?" There is no single answer that could accurately answer this. Some majors might teach you pertinent skills (i.e. business, computer science for software-based startups), however, nothing will teach you 100% of what you need to know.

(Continued)

Effective entrepreneurs are constantly learning new skills to respond to changing landscapes, and it is more important to be able to learn new skills than to have any particular skillset.

Myth #3: The idea is the most important part of a startup. You need to have an idea that is 100% unique

With 7 billion people on earth, there is probably someone else (or more likely multiple people) with an idea similar to yours. The ability to turn that idea into reality, and do so in a way that can make a profit, is MUCH more important than the idea itself. At 3DS programs that we teach, we sometimes encounter participants hesitant to share their ideas for fear of it being stolen. Our response is this: "No one is going to steal your stupid idea." If an idea is simple enough to be ripped off from an initial conversation, it probably wasn't that good of an idea to begin with. Further, the ability to validate an idea with customers, develop a business framework that can make money, and getting a product that customers will pay for to market is much more crucial than having something unique and new.

Practice > Theory

In theory, there is no difference between theory and practice

This slide is presented at all 3DS workshops, and reminds participants that things like customer acceptance and solid business fundamentals are more important than a unique idea.

(Continued)

(*Continued*)

Myth #4: All founders are young

Starting your own business is not a race against the clock. According to research by the Kauffman Foundation, the average age of founders in tech and high-growth industries was 40. Founders were also twice as likely to be over 55 than under 35 years old.[1]

Myth #5: A startup is not legitimate until it receives Venture Capital

It's understandable why Venture Capital receives a lot of attention and focus within entrepreneurship circles. Venture Capitalists, who are often rich and successful entrepreneurs themselves, are giving you money and trying to help your business succeed. Further, this money isn't a loan, and you don't have to pay it back (just give up some equity in your company). Subsequently, many see venture investment as free money to grow your business.

However, receiving an equity investment like Venture Capital is not all positive. As soon as you accept investment, you are no longer fully working for yourself, and instead working partially for these investors (and anyone else that owns equity in your startup). Further, these investors might have goals different from yours, and push you away from your ideal vision. Finally, raising funding takes a lot of time, which might be better spent building a business.

Not all startups are a good fit for Venture Capital. Some startups can be bootstrapped (grown with no outside investment, just reinvesting profits into growing a company), allowing founders to maintain all ownership. Also, Venture Capital is primarily focused on businesses that will provide a 10×–100× return on their investment in 3–5 years. If your business doesn't fit that profile, you might have a lot of trouble finding an investor. As a result, Venture Investment should not be pursued by default, and instead be carefully considered to see if it is a good match for your startup and its future goals. Because this myth (and the subsequent questions around Venture Capital) are so ubiquitous in the startup world, we discuss this idea in more detail in Chapter 5.

Dispelling these misconceptions will not tell you if entrepreneurship is or isn't for you. You will still have to figure that out for yourself, partially by using the questions in this chapter as a guide. However, this will help give you a more realistic picture of entrepreneurship, and help guide considerations about if you will fit in an entrepreneurial career.

investigates entrepreneurship education and learning. As you are reading through these questions, consider if one or more of these responses fits you, and what it might reveal about the suitability of an entrepreneurial career. We will also provide some color commentary to assist with these considerations.

1.3 Considerations for Entrepreneurial Careers

1.3.1 *How confident are you in your abilities to complete entrepreneurial tasks?*

a. I exude excellence for everything that I do. I can accomplish anything that I put my mind to.
b. I usually get things right. Even when I don't know the answer I can usually figure things out.
c. I don't know. Maybe, maybe not.
d. I don't like to do things I haven't done before or been taught specifically how to do.

There will be many times when there will be no single correct solution or course of action. Both founders and employees will have to make tough decisions, and own the outcomes of these decisions, good or bad. Many find this responsibility extremely enjoyable. Others find it overwhelming, and end up second-guessing themselves (c). Self-confidence is important when making these decisions. If (d) feels very familiar, the unpredictability that comes with entrepreneurship might be overwhelming for you.

Self-efficacy is a term used to describe one's belief in their ability to complete a particular task.[3] It is considered an important indicator of future entrepreneurship activity. Successful entrepreneurs need to be confident in their abilities, like the answers (a) and (b). While it's important to have confidence in one's own abilities, it is critical to not be overconfident (as in (a)), lest it cloud recognition of mistakes — sometimes you will not exude excellence, only mediocrity. Learning from these mistakes is a critical part of being lean, as it can help lead to iterative improvements. You must recognize and build on these mistakes, without letting it affect confidence in moving forward.

1.3.2 *How often do you meet deadlines set by yourself or others?*

a. Every single time. The thought of missing a deadline gives me a bit of an ulcer.
b. Most of the time. Sometimes things get delayed, but even then, I make it pretty close to the deadline.
c. To me, deadlines are more aspirational than binding.
d. If the task is enjoyable, yes. If not, all bets are off.
e. Usually I procrastinate long enough that it goes away. My kidney will stop hurting eventually.

As we mentioned above, many jobs within a startup have large degrees of independence. In order to properly utilize this freedom, successful entrepreneurs must have a sense of accountability. While (a) might be seen as a bit intense, deadlines should be important even when you don't have a boss/coworker dependent on you and checking in frequently. (b) is also a good response to this question, and accounts for some unpredictability that can come up for startup-related tasks.

Great entrepreneurs can effectively prioritize action items, and determine which ones are most critical to a business surviving and growing. (c) **might** be appropriate for some low-priority tasks. But for most actions, it's best to complete them in a timely manner. Further, when prioritizing efforts, it should be based on importance, and not enjoyability (d). If (e) is even remotely close to your response, it might be best to first see a doctor, then consider a different career field with more structure. While the independence that comes with entrepreneurship can be liberating for many, it requires a significant amount of self-discipline to manage this independence.

1.3.3 *Are you a perfectionist?*

a. Of course not. I am completely fine with imperfections, as they are noted in color-coded binders with a timeline for rectification on an hour-by-hour basis.

b. When others do something better than me, it feels like a failure.

c. "If you are not embarrassed by the first version of your product, you've launched too late."

d. I don't have time to make things perfect. I make things good enough.

Much of entrepreneurship is time management, and allocating your time to maximize impact in a couple of areas. Concepts like the Pareto Rule are common, and entrepreneurs must determine what will produce the most return on time invested. As a result, you usually cannot make things perfect, but good enough to be usable (d). (c) is actually a somewhat famous quote from Reid Hoffman, founder of LinkedIn, about perfectionism for the first release of your project. While intentionally a bit facetious, this quote does demonstrate the importance of releasing a product or service and getting user input to improve the next version, over trying to get every exact detail right the first time.

1.3.4 *You encounter a problem for your work and you have no clue how to solve it. What is your response?*

a. Try and turn it into someone else's problem. They are probably better at solving it than I would be.

b. Start googling things furiously until I find something resembling the answer.

c. Ask myself "what is the quickest way to come up with a good (but not perfect) solution. Try and come up with some quick experiments to actions to confirm initial hypothesis.

d. I can probably figure this out if I have to. But I'd rather have someone else do it, so I can focus on things that I know.

e. Curl up into a ball and freak out.

When starting a business, you are creating something that hasn't existed before. As a result, there will be many times when you will have to complete tasks or solve problems you haven't encountered previously. While responses like (a) and (d) can be appealing, entrepreneurs might not have the option to delegate challenges to someone else. Further, fear of new unknown situations cannot deter entrepreneurs (If (e) is an even remotely possible answer, entrepreneurship is not the right career for you). (b) and (c) are the best responses here, with (c) being slightly better in most situations. Entrepreneurship requires a lot of self-directed learning, and Google is a great tool for this. Further, time management can be important as well, and you will often have to ration time so that it can be allocated to many different areas. It is important to be able to not only solve unknown questions, but also do so in a way that leaves bandwidth for other efforts (we will introduce some business tools that can help with this in Chapter 10).

1.3.5 *Do any of the following scenarios make you apprehensive?*

a. Working on a startup for 6–12 months without salary.
b. Working on a business and having it fail with no financial return to show for it.
c. Working for below-market rate salary with limited/no benefits.
d. Having your job change dramatically in short amounts of time.

While the scenarios listed above may seem extreme, they are all actually fairly common occurrences for startups. While not guaranteed at every new venture, every new business has a fairly good chance of encountering one or more of the above scenarios. New businesses, even ones with revenue, are very often constrained on cash. Founders will frequently work for a time without salary as one of many efforts to keep costs down (a). While employees are usually paid, it is frequently below the market rate (the salary you could get for the same job at other companies), and with lower benefits (c). Although equity is typically included for these positions, this equity is typically illiquid (i.e. can't be sold/exchanged) for a long time, and from a purely financial standpoint, it usually does not make up for lower salary and benefits.

Great entrepreneurs are highly effective at assessing and managing risk. However, even when a business does everything right, it can still fail due to factors outside of its control. Entrepreneurs must have a low aversion to risk in order to deal with this reality.[5,6] While estimates vary, as many at 80% of startups fail, with founders not receiving a financial return that reflects their efforts (b). Also startups are frequently responding to additional information and customer feedback. This pivoting often involves changing job functions and responsibilities, causing employees to undertake responsibilities not originally outlined (d). To some people, this is a great thing — it keeps your job from getting boring or repetitive. Others prefer a more steady and regular work environment.

If any of these make you nervous or apprehensive, working for a startup might be too volatile for you. There might also be personal circumstances that discourage entrepreneurship as well. For example, raising children is expensive, and many parents need the salary a larger company will provide. For others, taking a job that doesn't provide health insurance is too risky and a dealbreaker. It's important to consider your personality and current situation when considering an entrepreneurial career.

1.4 Are You Still With Us?

If you've been reading through the previous questions, you might be thinking that entrepreneurship is not your true life's calling. If that's the case, it's good we put this chapter at the beginning — we just saved you ~160 pages of reading. Instead, use this time to go outside, surf the internet, or read another book on a different career path (I don't care — I'm a book, not your mother). One thing we frequently emphasize is "failing fast" — i.e. learning you are not on the correct path as quickly and cheaply as possible. If the time it took to read a single chapter convinced you that entrepreneurship is not a good fit, it should be considered an efficient use of time.

If you are feeling that entrepreneurship is not your optimal career choice, that does not represent a personal failure or shortcoming in any way. There is no single right or best answer to the question "Is entrepreneurship for you?" — there are many careers that are meaningful and highly impactful. Instead of viewing this question in the form of success/failure, you should view it in the context of good fit/bad fit, and finding a career path that is well matched to your personality. As with many things in life, there is no single right answer, or one choice that will be better than others.

As an example of this statement, consider the authors of this book. They look very stylish in crisp jeans and a 3DS t-shirt. However, this is not the case when these are swapped out for booty shorts and a halter top (don't worry, this example isn't visual). This doesn't mean that halter tops are a bad thing, or that the authors are personally deficient for not having legs like Catherine Bach. Further, people change over time — things that make you apprehensive now might not be highly concerning in the future. So if you find yourself hesitant about entrepreneurship, don't take it personally — it just means that we found your halter top, and it might be best to go shopping for a different outfit.

Another possible scenario is that you find yourself having mixed responses, with arguments for and against an entrepreneurial career. You might find some elements of entrepreneurship interesting, while knowing that being a founder or early startup employee is not your optimal career choice. There are alternative career paths that include entrepreneurial elements, without being fully immersed into a new venture. Some options that might work for people that fall into this category are elaborated as follows.

1.4.1 *Work for a "grown-up" startup*

One option is to work for what we call a "grown-up startup." We define these businesses as startups that have made it past the treacherous early stages of product/market fit — they probably have revenue, and might be somewhere close to profitability (usually they have raised funding at least once to get them to that milestone). Typically, these are businesses of 50–300 employees.

One factor of these businesses that appeals to many is that they have less volatility and risk than smaller startups. You probably won't have to work for no salary, or wonder if your next paycheck is going to bounce — you might even have some benefits. Also, their early days won't be too far in the past, and many appealing aspects of startup culture will still be present within the company. However, it won't feel **exactly** like a startup — there might be some elements that feel more like a corporate environment (like HR, annual employee evaluations, etc.). However, for many, this is a good mix of startup and stability, and can serve as a balance between the two.

1.4.2 *Find an innovative role within a large company*

Some large corporations embrace startup-style innovation in the hope of driving growth through new products and services. To accomplish this goal, they will create positions, and even entire divisions, with the mission to create innovative new products beyond traditional product lines. An example of this is Google X, which describes itself as a "moonshot factory" (pursuing ideas with a high level of risk, but have a very large payoff if successful). They pursue projects far from Google's search engine and advertising core, like self-driving cars and clean energy generation.[4]

These jobs are often described as working for a startup within a big company, and they appeal to many entrepreneurial-minded people. Many enjoy that these roles have much (but not all) of the autonomy and self-direction encountered at many startups. Also, job functions can evolve over time (like at a startup) they are typically less repetitive than traditional corporate jobs. One key difference is that because these jobs are located within a large company, they typically include more generous salaries and benefits than those offered by new or small businesses. Similar to working for a "Grown-Up" Startup, these jobs can be a good mix of startup and stability.

One challenge to pursuing one of these positions is that these jobs are not as common as they used to be (or should be). In the 70's and 80's, R&D labs like Xerox PARC or Bell Labs served as major drivers of innovation in the US. However, due to volatile returns, many companies downsized or got rid of these divisions, opting instead to innovate through acquisitions. As a result, these jobs can be hard to come across, with many more interested candidates than openings. If you are considering pursuing one of these positions, prepare for a highly competitive recruitment process.

1.4.3 *Come back to entrepreneurship later*

Entrepreneurship might not be the right choice for you **now**, but that doesn't mean it won't be at some point in the future. As we mentioned earlier, entrepreneurship does not have a shelf life, and there are more entrepreneurs over 55 than under 35. Most 3DS alumni do not start a venture immediately after completion of 3DS program. More often, they will return to entrepreneurship at a later time, when personal and professional circumstances are more amenable to these pursuits. It is completely acceptable to consider entrepreneurship as a future option, and in the present focus on developing skills that will help with this potential career path.

1.5 We Tried to Warn You — We Even Suggested a Few Alternatives

It you are still with us, congratulations on being persistent enough to make it through the entire chapter. This is a good thing. The term "grit" is used to describe the tenacity to not give up in tough situations. This resilience is believed by many to be a critical skill for all aspiring entrepreneurs.[2] Startup creation is never a purely forward procession, and as an entrepreneur, you will have to face challenges much more difficult than reading a book chapter. Grit helps effective entrepreneurs weather these challenges, and continue to work towards forward progress.

In the following chapters, we will introduce some actions one can undertake to develop skills important to entrepreneurship. These chapters can serve as a preliminary approach to this capability building. Further, this development is not an ending or one-time occurrence, and will be a continual process in your entrepreneurial career. However, we hope the rest of this book will provide a strong start for this journey.

References

1. Wolverson, R. (2013, March 4). The Best Age for a Start-Up Founder. *TIME*. Retrieved from https://business.time.com/2013/03/14/ask-the-expert-the-best-age-for-a-start-up-founder/.
2. Rosen, A. (2015, August 7). Why 'Grit' May Be Everything for Success. *Entrepreneur*. Retrieved from https://www.entrepreneur.com/article/247840.
3. Bandura, A. (1977). Self-efficacy: Toward a unifying theory of behavioral change. *Psychological Review, 84*(2), 191.
4. X. (2018). Retrieved from X, the moonshot factory: https://x.company/about.
5. Ekelund, J., Johansson, E., Järvelin, M. R., & Lichtermann, D. (2005). Self-employment and risk aversion — evidence from psychological test data. *Labour Economics, 12*(5), 649–659.
6. Caliendo, M., Fossen, F. M., & Kritikos, A. S. (2009). Risk attitudes of nascent entrepreneurs–new evidence from an experimentally validated survey. *Small Business Economics, 32*(2), 153–167.

Part 2
Customer-Based Startup Development

Chapter 2

Pre-Launch Customer Research

2.1 Introduction: Why Pre-Launch Research

Customer research is one of the first actions founders should undertake for their startup. It is a critical action that must be used to inform other early stages of startup development like product creation. When developing a product or service, there are many possible features or aspects to include — you can't include everything, and as the founder, you will have to choose which ones to prioritize. It is impossible to determine which of these will be most important to a customer without engaging them directly.

Further, companies that do not perform adequate customer research run the risk of creating products or services that ultimately become financial failures. Despite how advanced or novel a product is, it must solve a problem that customers are willing to pay for in order to be successful. For example, let's examine the Segway Personal Transporter. The product itself is impressive from a technological standpoint — it uses gyroscopes and automated controllers to be self-balancing while transporting people at up to 12 mph. However, despite this technological innovation there wasn't a significant customer segment for this product. The company only sold approximately 24,000 units in its first 5 years (the inventor Dean Kamen initially projected sales of 10,000 units per week). While there are some limited uses today, it is not the revolutionary transporter or automobile killer that many initially predicted it would be.[2]

Customer research can also help shape the business framework of your startup, and determine a model that will allow your startup to become profitable and financially sustainable. It is important to not only offer a product or service that solves a problem for customers, but also do so in a way that they will pay for. Customer engagement can determine important variables for a business framework like price, sales channels, and customer marketing strategies. When engaging customers, you will not only learn how they want to solve an important problem that they have, but also how they are willing to pay your business for said solution.

Further, some businesses are very hard or impossible to make profitable, through no fault of the founder. This can occur for a number of reasons — there might not be enough customers for a business to be profitable (one of the most common causes), or the solution offered might cost more to produce than customers are willing to pay. Sometimes technology is not developed fully to deliver the solution customers want. In any case, customer engagement can help you determine when a business idea is not viable before investing significant time or money into developing the concept. If you can quickly determine that a business is highly unlikely to be successful, this can be seen as a positive outcome (sometimes referred to as "failing fast"). By quickly determining that a business concept is not worth pursuing further, you can save time and resources for other entrepreneurial ventures that are more likely to succeed.

For all of these reasons, one of the most crucial actions for early-stage entrepreneurship involves interaction with potential customers. It is important to know your customer very well at all stages of company development, and you should undertake actions for this purpose as early as possible (and definitely before creating a product or service to sell to customers). Product development is expensive, and requires a lot of time and resources (more on this in the next chapter), and customer engagement helps ensure that these efforts are focused on solutions that are in-line with customer needs.

In this chapter, we will introduce some principles and techniques for customer research that should be utilized at the earliest stages of startup development. The focus of these actions will be to

Example: Don't Fall in Love with Your "Baby"

Some founders get very attached to their startup idea. This is understandable — they invest tons of time and other resources into its development, and it becomes a significant part of their daily life. While this passion can be an important driver of entrepreneurial action, it can also cause founders to become emotionally attached to a single embodiment of their business, and cause them to not want to change a single thing. However, this is undesirable, as startups are always evolving and improving as they learn more about the customers they are trying to sell to.

As a result, when facilitating 3DS programs, we sometimes say that a founder's startup is like their baby. In the eyes of new parents, their baby is the cutest one ever, and it is perfect in every way. While this is the sign of a loving parent, it is not completely accurate. Most babies are not the cutest in the world. Further, when their crying wakes them up in the middle of the night, even parents would agree their baby is far from perfect. However, if you were to mention this to a parent, they would probably be offended, and become defensive regardless of the accuracy of the critique. This sometimes happens with startups as well, and founders become defensive if you criticize any element of their venture.

It's ok to get attached to your startup idea, and feel very passionate about it, as one would a child. However, this attachment should not blind entrepreneurs to valid constructive criticism that can be used to improve their startup concept. It is important to not take it personally when a justified criticism emerges. This happens to every startup, and being able to channel negative feedback into positive growth is a sign of efficacy for an entrepreneur.

Customer input is one effective way to determine if they have an "ugly baby." The good news is, if your baby is ugly, customer research will help you determine ways to make it more attractive. This happens with almost all startups, and most successful startups started pursuing a different product/service than the one they end up settling on (for example, YouTube started out as a dating service before switching to a general video platform[1]). Further, if this research determines that the baby is really ugly, you can get rid of it and focus on a new one (don't try this with a real baby — the state will get mad — just trust us on this one). It is important to be mindful of this, and be open to adapting based on whatever findings may emerge from customer engagement.

learn as much as you can about your customers and the problems they have that they will pay your startup to solve. We will introduce how to determine likely customers for a startup, and different techniques to engage and learn from these likely customers. The results of these efforts can minimize the frequency and cost of mistakes in later stages of product or service development.

2.2 How to Determine "Likely Customers"

New businesses cannot sell to everyone all at once — they simply do not have the time or resources to pursue this approach. Further, for almost all businesses, there are some groups of people that are more likely to want or need a product or service that a business offers. As a result, every business has a group of "likely customers" that comprises of individuals most likely to give money to that business. For all customer engagement actions, it is important to only collect information from this segment.

Further, it can actually be detrimental to engage and learn from non-likely customers. These people will have different problems and needs than your likely customers, and their input might direct you away from an effective solution for paying customers. It is important that all customer research actions be aimed specifically at the identified likely customer.

An early step all founders must take in the pre-product customer research phase is determining who their segment of likely customers is. There is no single best way to determine the ideal customer segment for a business. Some choose based on who is easiest to pursue, or most likely to purchase the solution they are offering. Others choose the largest segment of customers with the greatest revenue potential. As the founder of a business, you must ultimately choose what you believe is best, as there are often multiple choices that could be considered the best choice of customer segment to pursue initially.

Further, the segment of likely customers should be highly specific. It can be tempting to define a customer segment as broadly as possible — this indicates a wider customer base and potential upside. However, a broadly defined customer segment will have more variance than a specifically defined one — it will be more difficult to identify customer needs that apply to the entire segment.

Example: Defining Likely Customers

When defining likely customers, one mistake founders sometimes make is selecting too broad a customer segment. The following are some examples that demonstrate how specific a customer segment should be for customer research actions. The left column corresponds to the type of business, while the middle column shows an overly broad customer segment that a business might choose. Finally, the right column shows a more specific customer segment.

Business Type	General Customer Segment (OK)	Specific Customer Segment (Better)
A shoe store	Everyone with feet	Women aged 24–35 looking for chic shoes for nightlife.
A tech company that helps customers find paid parking	Everyone who drives a car	People who live or work in car-dense areas (i.e. downtown in large cities) that purchase parking 5–7 times a week but don't rent monthly parking spaces.
A grocery delivery service	Everyone who buys groceries	Single professionals that work 50+ hours/week, and eat outside of their home/apartment less than twice/week.
A company developing an app that helps pet owners find boarding services	Everyone that owns a pet	Dog owners that travel out of town more than 21 days/year and spend >$2,000 annually on their pets.

When you select a specific customer segment, it doesn't mean that you will turn away business from customers outside of that segment. It just means that you have determined the group of people that you believe are most likely to become paying customers for your business, and that your customer research actions will focus on these individuals. As a founder, time is a scarce commodity, and correctly defining a likely customer segment helps ensure that customer research efforts are exclusively for likely paying customers.

This will also affect potential solutions resulting from engaging this broad segment, and they will be less likely to align with customer needs. As a result, identifying broad customer segments can actually be a disservice that lowers the accuracy and value of subsequent customer research actions.

It is possible that a startup will have more than one likely customer segment. In this case, it is a good idea to choose a single segment to focus on at first. Startups are often constrained by resources and time, and it is better to fully focus on a single customer segment than partially on two different segments. However, this is not a permanent status, and as your startup grows, you can expand to focus on additional customer segments. Further, if a customer segment turns out to be less promising than previously thought, you can switch to another segment that might be more promising.

Finally, a segment of likely customers selected initially might not be as promising as initially thought. Customer engagement can reveal various reasons why this might be the case — the customer segment might not be as large as initially believed, or the problem this segment wants solved is not the one you initially envisioned. At this early stage of startup development, no decision is set in stone, and can change to account for additional findings. As we stated earlier, founders should not "fall in love with their baby" and be willing to adjust if a better opportunity presents itself in a different segment of likely customers.

2.2.1 *Users vs. Customers*

For many businesses, those who purchase from the business and those who use the product/service are the same person. However, there are other situations where the end user is different from the person who purchases the product or service. For example, for businesses that sell products for young children, the user is the child, whereas the customer is the child's parents who purchase products for their children. As another example, people that have Facebook accounts are users, while the customers are the advertisers that buy ad space from the company. While it is important to understand

This picture of 3DS participants speaking with customers directly has been shown at every 3DS program since 2010. Learning by immersion in experiences is at the core of 3DS and will always remain this way.

users, customers are more important for a business, since they are the ones that will bring money into the business (which we have stated previously, is critical for all businesses to survive).

Ideally, an entrepreneur will conduct extensive primary research with both users and customers. However, when the inevitable time constraints do come up, it is best to prioritize customers. These are the people that will bring money into a business, which is critical for every business in order to be financially sustainable. Fortunately, the techniques introduced in this chapter can be used to learn from both users and customers, and founders do not need to learn a second set of skills if this dynamic exists for their business.

2.3 Primary Research

The best way to learn from customers is to engage them directly (referred to in this chapter as "Primary research"). Fortunately, there is no special skill or ability needed for this action, and anyone can successfully conduct primary research once they have identified their target customer segment.

2.3.1 *Interviews*

Interviews with likely customers are one of the most widely used techniques that founders use during pre-launch customer research. This entails having a conversation with an interview subject (someone who falls in the definition of "likely customers") about a problem their startup is hoping to solve. When conducted correctly, it gives founders a first-hand look into the mindset of their likely customers, and how they interact with a problem (and attempt to solve it).

The topics of these interviews should focus on what problems the customers experience most, and what kinds of solutions they would like to see. Questions should be prepared beforehand, so that all interviews ask about similar themes. This allows the customer research to identify trends and themes that are common among multiple likely customers (this can serve as a strong indicator of demand for a specific feature for a product or service).

Capturing stories from likely customers is another technique sometimes used during customer interviews. Detailed stories can be an effective method to convey feelings, priorities, and other pertinent information from a likely customer. Further, encouraging a likely customer to share stories can be an effective way to get them to open up, or talk about their experiences in a way that generates meaningful insights for you. As a result, some interview questions can be designed to encourage the interview subject to tell stories.

Customer interviews are conducted in "real time," which means both the interviewing and interviewed parties must share information at the same time. This can be challenging for some customer segments, and some effort must go into identifying and engaging interview subjects. However, this can be advantageous as well, as it allows the interviewer to go "off script" and explore topics not brainstormed previously. If the interview subject mentions something particularly interesting, the conversation can focus on that response, and go into more detail. Interviews allow for follow-up questions that can build on previous remarks. Further, even with extensive planning for interview questions, there are often topics that a founder will not think of. Interviews allow you to learn about these topics, possibly preventing mistakes down the road. This is one particularly powerful feature of interviews, and makes up for the extra effort needed to conduct them in real time.

Interviews do not have to be conducted in person. Many founders get creative, and use various forms of technology (i.e. Google, Facebook, LinkedIn, etc.) to identify and reach out to interview subjects. Further, they can use technology (i.e. phone, Skype, Zoom, WhatsApp, etc.) to conduct these interviews as well. The most important consideration for customer interviews is that they are engaging someone within the segment of previously determined likely customers. Subsequently, any approach that successfully and accurately contacts these individuals is acceptable.

2.3.2 *Surveys*

Sometimes, it can be difficult to interview a large set of potential customers (due to geography, availability, etc.). One solution for this is to use surveys instead of interviews as a method of primary engagement for customers. A survey is a questionnaire distributed to individuals. Surveys have the advantage that they don't have to be completed in real time like interviews do, and offer more flexibility for collecting input from likely customers. They can be distributed to a wider audience (especially true when using an online survey tool like Google Forms), and require less effort to engage likely customers than interviews do.

Surveys are typically shorter than interviews are, and take less time to complete. They typically do not collect as much information as interviews do as well. Further, they do not allow for follow up questions or going off script like interviews do, allowing for less opportunity for unexpected findings.

Finally, surveys often ask questions that have multiple choice or quantifiable answers. This can make it easier to analyze and interpret a large set of survey responses. For example, one common survey question used asks respondents how much they spend to solve [Problem experienced]. The average of all responses can provide insights about how much individuals within a likely customer segment spend on solutions to a problem a startup is trying to solve. Another common question type asks how important a certain feature or function is to them with multiple choice responses (typically ranging from "Very important" to "Very unimportant"). Questions like these can help the survey administrator determine how prominent a problem is, and whether it is worth emphasizing in a potential product or service.

Ultimately, founders must determine for themselves whether surveys or interviews are better for customer research. This decision will be based on who their likely customer segment is, and what topics they need to learn more about for their startup. Further, many founders will use both when conducting pre-launch customer research (surveys to reach a wide variety of likely customers, and interviews to explore some topics in depth). It is not necessary to choose one or the other for pre-launch customer research.

Examples of Survey and Interview Questions

The questions you ask during this direct customer engagement will directly determine how much you learn from these efforts. Subsequently, it is important to plan what questions you will ask in an interview or survey before doing to. Below are some examples of effective interview and survey questions for early-stage customer research, as well as some elaboration on what the questions want to learn, and why they are effective.

In this example, all questions are written for a startup that is looking to help people purchase clothing online. They have already determined their likely customer segment to be men and women aged 25–40, who identify themselves as "tech-savvy." However, they also have difficulty shopping for clothing online, despite their willingness to do so.

(*Continued*)

Examples of Interview Questions

Do you ever shop for clothes online?
What do you like/dislike about shopping for clothes online?
What do you like/dislike about shopping for clothes in person?

These questions aim to better understand how likely customers shop for clothing. Further, they are intentionally written to be open ended, and allow the interview subject to talk about what they like or don't like, and tell stories. They would also likely lead to opportunities to go "Off-script" and ask follow-up questions based on their initial response.

Have you ever paid for a service to help you find clothing to buy?
(If Yes, ask the following questions),
How much did you pay for this service?
What was the name of this product/service?
What did you like or dislike about this service?

These questions examine how likely customers have attempted to solve a problem previously. Asking how much likely customers have paid in the past might be helpful for determining the pricing. Further, by asking what their customers have done in the past, they can learn about potential competitors, and how the startup can differentiate itself from these competitors in a way that will be successful.

Example Survey Questions

How many items do you typically buy when you go clothes shopping at a brick and mortar store?
How many different stores do you typically visit when you go clothes shopping?
How long do you typically spend in a store while clothes shopping?

These questions are trying to learn shopping habits and preferences of their likely customers. Results from these questions can be used to help a startup shape a solution that fits with these preferences. While these questions could lead to open ended stories and responses, they will probably not collect as many insights as they would if asked during an interview.

(*Continued*)

(Continued)

Please rate the following actions based on how important they are for you when deciding to purchase an item of clothing.

	Not Important	Slightly Important	Moderately Important	Important	Very Important
Being able to try on clothes before buying.	1	2	3	4	5
Seeing clothing items paired with other items.	1	2	3	4	5
Having a stylist/store employee recommend garments to you.	1	2	3	4	5
Having help finding the best size/fit of clothing for your body type.	1	2	3	4	5
Being able to easily compare an item to similar ones to consider for purchase.	1	2	3	4	5

This question block helps the startup learn what features are most important to their likely customer segment. Further, by asking the question in this format, you can get a numerical score of all features (the average of all responses), and determine which ones are most important for a potential solution.

As a final thought, many of the same questions can be asked in either surveys or interviews in an attempt to learn the same things. However, there are slight differences in how these questions would be worded for use in each format. When preparing for customer research, it is important to not only think of what you want to learn from your customer, but what medium you will be using to do so.

2.3.2.1 *Avoid leading questions*

When conducting primary research, you want to be as objective as possible, and to receive honest feedback about your idea, even if it is negative. However, this does not always happen, and entrepreneurs sometimes make the mistake of asking leading questions when conducting primary research. These are questions that prompt the respondent to answer in a particular way. Humans take cues from those they are interacting with, even during verbal conversations. Subsequently, how you ask a question can influence how the person answers.

Some leading questions will plant an idea in the head of the person being interviewed, prompting them to give an inaccurate answer that affirms what you already believe, even if this is not true in reality. Other leading questions try to implicitly sell an idea or solution to the person being asked. This could lead to them expressing a need for a solution that they might not want when not prompted to do so. In all embodiments, leading questions are detrimental to the customer research process because they lower the accuracy and quality of the feedback you receive during this process. These responses will make you feel like you are onto something, and that customer research confirms what you previously thought about a product idea. However, this will not be the case in reality, and when it comes time to sell your product or service, the predicted customer demand will not be there. Remaining objective during primary customer research gives you the best chance of collecting accurate customer insights, and using these insights to offer a product or service that will ultimately lead to paying customers.

Example: Avoiding Leading Questions

Leading questions are highly undesirable because you want to be as objective as possible when conducting primary research with customers. Even if unintentional, they can produce inaccurate insights about likely customers, the problems they experience, or potential solutions you are trying to develop. Below are some examples of leading questions, as well as explanations why they are leading/not good for customer engagement. We also provide examples of how to reword these questions to collect objective information from likely customers.

(*Continued*)

(Continued)

Leading Question	A Better Question to Ask
Wouldn't you like an app that shows you where to find open parking spots on a map? (This question assumes that the user wants to use a map-based app to find parking spots as a solution.)	What don't you like about finding parking spots? Is there any technology you think would help with this process?
How many times a day do you forget to reply to emails? What do you need to remember to reply to especially important messages? (This question assumes that forgetting emails is a problem, and likely customers need a solution that gives them reminders.)	Do you ever forget to reply to important emails? Have you ever tried to set reminders for yourself? What does or doesn't work?
How much would you pay for a subscription service for your pet's food? What other items would you subscribe to receive regularly? (This question assumes that customers want a subscription service, and they might subscribe for other products as well.)	Do you ever forget to buy recurring items for your pets? How do you currently remember to do so?

Remember, the goal of customer engagement isn't to defend your idea, or sell it to others. You want to receive objective information on what products and services customers are willing to pay for to solve a problem that they have. Further, you don't want to create a falsely optimistic sense of demand for a certain solution that customers want. Either way, when planning for customer research or interviews, watch out for leading questions, and always work to make sure your questions are as objective as possible.

2.3.3 *Other primary customer research actions — customer observation*

While customer interviews and surveys comprise a vast majority of customer research actions, they are not the only techniques businesses can employ to learn from likely customers. Businesses will sometimes perform observation studies (either by filming a likely customer, or observing them in-person), where they will view their subject going through a set of actions or processes. While not as common as the previously described approaches, they can sometimes provide insights into the customer experience that would be difficult to learn elsewhere.

Observation studies can be effective because they collect unfiltered information from the subject being observed. These studies will sometimes convey insights that a user doesn't realize or can't articulate during an interview. Further, observing a likely customer can help elaborate how they might interact with a potential solution and the environment in which they encounter the problem a founder is trying to solve.

While observation studies can be insightful, they require extra planning and preparation to be completed successfully. Before being undertaken, the founder must brainstorm what to look for, and what questions they want to answer. Further they must ensure that the method of observation does not distract the person being observed, or distort how they normally complete actions. Despite this extra effort, they are not guaranteed to produce insights that couldn't otherwise be obtained from interviews and surveys. As a result, most entrepreneurs stick to a combination of customer interviews and surveys when performing customer research actions.

2.4 Secondary Research

Secondary research entails looking at research conducted by others. Examples of secondary research include industry reports, news articles, databases, government records, etc.

While secondary research can be beneficial, there are some reasons why it is not as informative as primary research. First, secondary research might not match the exact customer segments a founder is studying. Further, it might focus on areas or problems that are separate from what they are solving. As a result, the key insights from secondary research might not be directly applicable to a startup or likely customer segment.

Further, secondary research cannot be used for iterative product development. A secondary research source represents a snapshot of an industry or customer segment. However, new businesses are often changing based on feedback from customers. Subsequently, primary research is required to maximize the quality and time-efficiency of customer development efforts.

Secondary research should be seen as a supplement for primary research instead of a replacement. It can be good for giving an overview of overall themes like market trends, new technologies, and growth areas. However, it rarely informs you of what a startup's specific customers want, and cannot accurately guide a business's customer development strategy on its own.

2.5 Conclusion

In this chapter, we discuss how founders can learn about their customers before creating a product or service. The best way to learn about customers is to engage them directly. It is important to identify likely customers, and only target them for primary research and engagement. However, when doing so, there are a variety of methods to follow, and founders have some opportunity to choose the method that works best.

Many of the approaches in this chapter are meant to minimize mistakes, and the amount of time and effort needed to adjust or pivot to be more in line with what your customers want. While customer engagement can help pre-empt many of these mistakes, it will never be 100% effective. As a startup gains more information, it will identify opportunities to improve based on this increased information. It is a matter of when this pivot will occur, not if. Still, this customer research remains important, as it will minimize mistakes and the need to pivot as much as possible.

Finally, the authors are often asked how much customer research is too much. While the answer varies somewhat from business to business, there are very few startups that collect "too much" customer input. Conducting too little customer research is a much more common occurrence. A more appropriate question would be to ask how to disperse customer research actions. These actions are not only completed before launching a product or service, but continue to take place during the product development cycle, and after product launch. In the next chapter, we will discuss later stages of customer research, and ways to continue to collect customer input at later stages of a business life cycle.

References

1. Nieva, R. (2016, March 14). YouTube started as an online dating site. *CNET*. Retrieved from https://www.cnet.com/news/youtube-started-as-an-online-dating-site/.
2. Schneider, J., & Hall, J. (2011, April). Why Most Product Launches Fail. *Harvard Business Review*. Retrieved from https://hbr.org/2011/04/why-most-product-launches-fail.

Chapter 3

Iterative Prototyping and Product Development for Startups

In the last chapter, we discussed how to collect input from customers before starting to create a product or service for your startup. This is an important step to prepare for creating what your business will sell. If done correctly, this research will identify a need or problem that your customers have, and what your business can provide to them in exchange for payment.

Once you have completed pre-launch customer research, you can begin to pivot your focus towards creating a solution for your customers (in this setting, a "solution" can refer to either a product or service that you offer). The process for this is similar to the one that we described in the last chapter. Once again, user feedback is crucial to creating a successful product or service (i.e. one that customers will buy). As a result, your interactions with likely customers do not end, and you will continue to engage them. Further, this approach will be iterative, and you will test your solutions with customers, and use their feedback to make small, incremental improvements while developing the product or service you will ultimately sell to customers.

In this chapter, we will discuss how to use findings from pre-launch customer research for product development. We will introduce the concept of prototypes, and how they can be used to gain additional valuable feedback from users/customers. We will also describe various ways to construct prototypes, test them with users/ customers, and gain valuable feedback to improve their designs. These steps fit into an overall iterative, incremental process that is employed to successfully create solutions that customers will ultimately pay for.

3.1 Prototypes

Prototypes are used to help startups develop and gain insights on a potential solution they will offer to customers. While the term "prototype" has many different uses in various applications, in this embodiment, it is anything that conveys an idea or feature for the purpose of testing and gaining user feedback (In this chapter, we are primarily discussing prototypes for user testing). It is used to collect feedback on potential solutions that can be used to improve future designs. It is an important tool for early-stage startups, as it allows their potential customers and end users to interact with potential solutions. This allows a startup to collect input that couldn't be collected solely through primary customer engagement.

Further, new businesses have many unanswered questions and unknowns, even after completing extensive customer research. Prototype construction and testing is a great way to address this uncertainty, and turn "I think" into "I know" for many of these questions through additional customer engagement. However, at this stage, you should have a better idea of what problem your defined segment of likely customer's experiences, and employ this knowledge into a prototype solution that will attempt to address this problem. As a result, while it remains important to focus on customers and their needs, the way you do this will be different from the customer engagement techniques introduced in the previous chapter.

3.1.1 *Iterative prototype development:*
The Build → Test → Learn cycle

Prototype construction and testing is an iterative process, roughly divided into three stages. The first stage is Build, where a concept for a solution is selected and a prototype based on this concept is created. Selecting a concept should rely substantially on previously completed customer research. The next stage is Test, where this prototype is presented to potential end users and customers. They interact with this prototype, and share their reactions and opinions based on this interaction. A founder will collect these responses from multiple test subjects, leading to observations and insights. Finally, founders will synthesize what they have learned (Learn), leading to new ideas of how to improve the overall concept. This can entail modifications to the current concept, or starting over and selecting one that is completely new. However, once this cycle is completed, it starts over again. Subsequently, prototyping should not be seen as a single linear process, but one that is cyclical and builds on iterative improvements.

3.1.2 *Early stage prototypes*

The key to an effective prototype is to create something that allows you to collect feedback from customers and end users. Subsequently, prototypes do not have to look or act like the final product or service that a startup will offer to customers in order to be effective. In fact, it is often preferable to make a prototype that does not resemble the final product, as it allows you to create prototypes more quickly and cheaply. This leaves more time for testing and user feedback, and more opportunities to repeat the Build $\rightarrow$ Test $\rightarrow$ Learn cycle. This can be especially true for early stage prototypes, which are created when founders tend to have fewer customer insights and more unknowns.

The term "low-fidelity" is sometimes used to describe prototypes that are simple, low-tech, and created with minimal resources. Low-fidelity prototypes can be highly informative, and can provide almost as much feedback as ones of higher complexity. Further, because they can be made in a fraction of the time of fully functional ones, they are more efficient on a time/insight basis than those of higher complexity.

Low-fidelity prototypes should be used almost exclusively during the early stages of product development. At this time, founders still have many unknowns about the solution they will ultimately offer to customers. Subsequently, the solution they are developing is likely to change significantly in the future as they obtain further insights. Low Fidelity prototypes help shorten the Build → Test → Learn cycle, allowing you to more quickly obtain these insights, answer these unknowns, and update your solution to be more in line with customer sentiment.

Examples of Low-Fidelity Prototypes for Startups

As we stated earlier, prototypes do not have to closely resemble the final product or service offered by a business. There are diverse ways to quickly produce prototypes for testing. Some of the most frequently employed methods for creating low-fidelity prototypes are elaborated as follows.

Wizard of Oz prototype — A Wizard of Oz prototype is one that simulates functionality for an end user, without creating an actual working concept. It is based on the scene in the eponymous movie where the wizard pretends to have a working autonomous giant head, while really controlling everything with levers behind the scenes. By simulating functionality, you can save time and resources required to create a working prototype, without changing the experience of the end user (which is most important for obtaining high-quality feedback).

These prototypes are particularly useful for a complex or time-consuming product or service. Many successful businesses used this type of prototype to validate their business concept (for example, in the early days of Zappos, instead of creating a costly inventory and warehouse system, the founder would wait for an order, then go to the store and purchase that item to ship to customers. Although this method was not how the business would ultimately operate, it did prove that people would buy shoes online, which was a crucial condition for Zappos to have paying customers and ultimately to be successful).[1]

(*Continued*)

(Continued)

Storyboards — A storyboard uses a series of sketches or pitches to demonstrate a user's experience or process that occurs over time. Storyboards can be useful for prototyping services, or items that customers interact with in differing ways. Further, by communicating visually, it can sometimes demonstrate a concept in ways that text alone cannot. You do not have to be a highly skilled or trained artist to produce storyboards, and many founders build and test storyboards by using simple sketches like stick figures.

Paper prototypes for software and mobile apps — Prototypes for software and mobile apps do not have to include computer code. In fact, many startups will instead use paper prototypes to save the time and costs required to create functional software. These prototypes can collect much of the feedback functioning software can, while being made for a fraction of the time and cost. Paper prototypes are highly effective for iterative product development as well — some startups will make high-quality paper prototypes in ~30 minutes. Along with testing and analyzing, they can perform multiple rounds of iterative development in a single day. A google search for "iPhone paper prototype template" or "Android paper prototype" will turn up many images that can serve as a template for these prototypes.

Wireframes — Wireframes are prototypes used for websites and other interactive technology. They present the content displayed on various pages, the structure of these pages, and overall layout of the user interface. They are used to test how users interact with a product, and how they navigate between various elements. As with paper prototypes, they do not focus on the working properly, and instead prioritize gaining end user feedback. There are many free and low-cost wireframe tools available, including (but not limited to) Wireframe. cc, MockFlow, Pencil Project, InVision, etc.[2]

3.1.3 *Prototypes of increasing complexity*

Up until now, we have primarily discussed low-fidelity prototypes that are fast and simple to make. This is intentional, as early on, founders should focus on short, fast rounds of prototype creation and testing. However, for later stages of concept development, this can change, and prototypes can have increasing complexity.

There are multiple reasons for shifting towards the creation of more advanced prototypes. Eventually, a founder will reach the limit of what can be learned from low-fidelity prototypes, and will want to further refine or perfect a concept that has previously received positive customer feedback. Other times, later stage prototypes attempt to build and test functionality, to ensure a final offering will work with customers. Finally, some prototypes can start planning for manufacturing, and help founders better understand how to produce a product they will sell to customers.

Many founders wonder about how much complexity should go into later stage prototypes. Once again, there is no single answer to this question, and it is up to a founder to determine what is the best use of time and other resources. Generally, prototypes gradually become more complex over multiple cycles of creating and testing (instead of making large jumps from low-fidelity to high-fidelity prototypes). However, you should note that as prototypes become more complex, they require more time and effort to make modifications. As a result, founders should be aware to not rush into ramping up prototype complexity, and be willing to wait until they have some insights from previous prototyping stages to do so.

3.2 Testing Prototypes

Once a prototype is constructed, it must be used to gain additional feedback from likely customers. The process for obtaining this feedback is prototype testing, where likely customers interact with a prototype, and provide their thoughts on the product.

Prototype testing allows founders to learn about their likely customers beyond what they might share in an interview or survey. Sometimes, likely customers can't articulate the problem they have, which can sometimes be addressed through prototype testing. Other times, they might not realize a particular feature or need as important. As a result, even though prototype testing can take more time than customer engagement, they can also provide insights not otherwise attainable. Subsequently, during testing, it is important that a prototype is not just shown to a likely customer, and that they actually interact with it in a realistic use case. This allows founders to collect the maximum amount of information available from their prototypes.

Further, it is important that this testing only occur with likely customers and end users. Doing otherwise would lead to feedback that can be inaccurate and non-applicable to your startup's customers. However, the good news is that by this point, you have already identified specific likely customers, and have experience engaging this population from previous customer research actions. Building on this experience will help lower the time needed to find likely customers for prototype testing.

3.2.1 *Planning for prototype testing*

Before testing a prototype, you should plan what you want to learn during this testing phase. You should plan how you will collect this information as well. Observation while your end user is interacting with a prototype is a primary method of learning. However, you must determine what to look for, and how you might measure various aspects of user interaction (i.e. how many times do they press a specific button, how they navigate through a website, etc.). You can also use post-interaction interviews and surveys to capture additional insights from your test subjects. These questions will also be influenced by what you designate as most important for prototype testing.

The following are some topics you can consider when preparing for prototype testing.

What is currently unknown, that I can learn from testing a prototype?
Even after thorough customer research, you will not know everything needed about your startup's customers. Prototype testing is another opportunity to address these unknowns, and improve your knowledge of customers which is crucial to a startup's success.

Does the prototype solve the problem customers have?
Customers buy products to solve significant problems they have. In the last chapter, we stressed the importance of identifying these problems, and saving potential solutions for later. When testing prototypes, however, you also want to ensure that you provide an effective solution to your customers. Solving a problem for paying customers is a key to business sustainability, and prototype testing often focuses on this topic.

Do likely customers use the product as intended?
Sometimes when testing prototypes, end users might not understand a product as well as a founder/creator might. This is understandable — they have not put nearly as much effort or thought into the solution as you have. Also, new concepts can be challenging to understand the first time they interact with it. They might not understand how a prototype works right away. It is important to learn if users/customers need a tutorial or other orientation to a solution — if they don't understand it, it is unlikely they will buy it. This can be addressed with tutorials or instructions for likely customers, which can also be a part of prototype testing.

Always Be Objective When Testing Prototypes
In the last chapter, we mentioned that you should not be afraid to receive negative feedback from potential customers. This concept applies to prototypes as well. The objective of prototype testing is not to sell or defend your idea, but to receive feedback that improve future prototypes and solutions (don't worry, selling will come later). Instead, think of testing as a chance to improve your solution to keep customers satisfied with what your startup offers. In Chapter 2, we warned you not to fall in love with your "baby," which can also happen with founders that put a lot of time and effort into creating prototypes. Further, you should be open to adapting your prototype as you learn from testing with likely customers. Making multiple quick, incremental improvements is more efficient than a few large ones, and can help minimize the amount of time and resources spent on ineffective solutions.

3.3 Creating an Initial Offering for Customers: The Minimum Viable Product

The process of creating and testing prototypes, in addition to providing valuable customer input, helps startups gradually advance towards creating the product or service they will ultimately offer to customers. However, a startup cannot create all product features initially, and must prioritize what should go into the initial product released to customers. Some features are critical to customer satisfaction, while others are less important and therefore a lower priority. One major milestone in this overall process is creation of the first offering that is available to customers.

A Minimum Viable Product (MVP) is the minimum functionality or set of features that a product or service needs to satisfy early customers. It allows a startup to get their product or service to customers as early as possible. Further, an MVP is often the first time a startup earns revenue from customers. This makes it an important tool to test the business model of a startup, providing input in areas like pricing, sales channels, and marketing communications.

As an example of an MVP, consider Gmail, the email service provided by Google. Launched in 2004, users can now integrate their email account with many other Google products like Calendar, Drive, and Docs, as well as other productivity tools like Asana and Slack. However, most of these features were not included in the initial product release. The MVP for Gmail included the ability to login from any web browser, the ability to send and receive email, and 1 GB of storage (much more than what other competitors offered at that time). Once the product was released and validated with users, Google later gradually added many additional features to the product. These additions were often based on feedback from account holders or data about how they were using their Gmail accounts.

3.3.1 *Deciding what should be included in an MVP*

The first step for creating an MVP is to determine the features (in this case, defined as parts of the overall product or service) that will go into this creation. To do this, reference the findings and insights obtained from previously completed customer research and prototype testing. It is highly likely that some specific problem or trend was mentioned by most or all of likely customers engaged during these actions. Subsequently some features or functionality might emerge as most effective to address the problem customers want to solve. These should stand out as important features that should be considered for inclusion in an MVP. If previous stages of customer engagement were performed correctly, there should be a dearth of findings to reference for this action. If this is not the case (which *can* happen, even when comprehensive customer research was completed), it is acceptable to complete additional customer engagement to gain further clarity.

It is also prudent to consider the feasibility of creating possible features, and if their significance aligns with ease of implementation. It might be overly time- or resource-consuming to create a particular feature, which could detract from other aspects of the MVP. Even if a feature is highly desirable to customers, if it costs too much to create, it might have to wait until later development cycles. As a founder, you will have to judge the cost-benefit analysis of particular features and whether they should be included in an MVP.

When deciding on features for an MVP, you shouldn't feel compelled to include as many features as possible. Creating and releasing an MVP does not mean that you cannot add additional features in the future. You should consider an MVP as the first product that you release to customers, and a way to utilize time and other resources for constructing the most crucial elements of a product. In the future, when these are less scarce, you can build upon your MVP with additional features and improvements.

It is also important to note that Minimum Viable Product should not be confused with a low-quality product. Even if you limit the features contained in an MVP, you should not reduce the quality of the features that are released. This can hurt the perception of your startup, deterring future customers.[3] However, this also does not mean that you should wait until all elements of the MVP are perfect before releasing it to customers. Once again, we will reference the (slightly exaggerated) Reid Hoffman quote "If you are not embarrassed by the first version of your product, you've launched too late." Instead, you should release an MVP when it is "good enough" for your customers.

3.3.2 *Obtaining customer feedback from an MVP*

Releasing an MVP does not signal the end of collecting feedback from customers, and you should continue to engage them even after you begin collecting revenue. This feedback will provide information on customer needs, and continue the process of incrementally improving your startup. There are various ways to collect this feedback. Some startups will send surveys to their customers, while others might build assessment tools into a product in order to collect information automatically (for example, a startup might count how many times various pages within a website are accessed, or what page navigation route is most frequently used). While there is no single way to collect this information, a startup should have a strong understanding of what it wants to measure and why.

Further, MVPs can provide crucial customer validation in the form of whether customers will actually buy a product. This is crucial, since startups need paying customers to survive, and lack of paying customers is the leading cause of startup failure. While this validation is similar to that obtained during previous customer engagement work, it goes beyond what can be learned from an interview or survey, and can provide a more accurate assessment of customer demand for a product or service.[4]

Right now, you might be wondering why this validation is so crucial when primary customer research focuses on the same area. No primary customer research can prove customer demand with 100% certainty. Humans are erratic, which can affect the responses they provide during interviews and surveys. Sometimes people will answer a question inaccurately (even when they don't intend to do so). Other times, they might overestimate how much they might be willing to pay for a solution. Getting a customer to give you money is one of the strongest forms of customer validation a startup can receive, and one key function of the MVP is to obtain this validation, or help founders learn how to change their product into one that can.

However, this also doesn't decrease the importance of the customer engagement we introduced in Chapter 2 — this work is crucial to get to the stage where you can create and release an MVP (if you were to skip this step, creating an MVP would essentially be guesswork, which is not an efficient use of time or resources). A product is much more likely to resonate with paying customers if it is created based on their feedback. Finally, creating a product takes significantly more time than an interview or survey with likely customers. It is much more efficient to conduct customer research before creating an MVP, as it lowers the chance and amount of costly, time-consuming mistakes.

3.4 Conclusion

In this chapter, we discussed how to build on findings from customer research, and begin constructing a product or service that you will offer to customers. While the focus will continue to be on customer needs, we moved beyond learning of a problem these customers have, to trying to come up with a solution to these problems. We also introduced prototype construction and testing as a means of testing potential solutions. All of this effort leads to the first offering to customers, an MVP.

The Build → Learn → Test cycle that we introduced in this chapter is important for effective product creation regardless of industry and what you offer to customers. This cycle continues even after you release an MVP to customers (for example, after buying something, how many times are you asked to review a product, or fill out a survey about your shopping experience)? You should never stop collecting input. However, this cycle will depend on what kind of product or service your startup offers. For example, it is easy to make quick updates to software and webpages. However, if your business sells a physical product that is produced by an outside manufacturer, it will take a bit longer to make product updates. While the length of this cycle will vary, the iterative nature of development and improvement is consistent.

Finally, you might find yourself striving to make a perfect product or service for your customers. It is important to remind yourself that this perfection is elusive and difficult to achieve. However, this is not a deterrent, and every startup starts with an imperfect product that they improve over time. As long as you are open to responding to feedback from your customers, and making improvements, you can create a product or service for your customers that can ultimately be successful.

References

1. Hsieh, T. (2010, May 17). How Zappos was Born: Place Bets on Passionate People. *Harvard Business Review*. Retrieved from https://hbr.org/2010/05/how-zappos-was-born-place-bets.
2. Hufford, B. (2019, October). 11 Best Forever Free Wireframing Tools for Designers (2021). *Clique*. Retrieved from https://cliquestudios.com/free-wireframing-tools/.
3. *The Downside of Applying Lean Startup Principles*. (2018, September 28). Retrieved from Knowledge@Wharton: https://knowledge.wharton.upenn.edu/article/the-limitations-of-lean-startup-principles/.
4. Reis, E. (2011). *The Lean Startup*. New York: Crown Business, pp. 1–336.

Chapter 4

Entrepreneurship Canvases

4.1 Introduction

One of the authors recently met with an entrepreneur who participated in a 3 Day Startup (3DS) program a decade ago. Since participating in this program, he has become a serial entrepreneur, and
was currently working on his third company. He shook the author's
hand and thanked him — not for the great community of people or
the talented facilitator that ran the 3DS program he participated in,
but for introducing him to the Lean Canvas. He stated that this tool
kept him working on the right challenges all throughout his entrepreneurial journey.

The rise of the Internet is a truly magical thing. It has brought
about a massive change in what is needed to start a company. Before
the internet, entrepreneurs had to perform more of the costly,
capital-intensive tasks — such as leasing a brick-and-mortar store, or
hiring employees — before launching. However, it was not just the
financial outlay that was constraining. Other tasks, such as performing market research, identifying potential partners, and establishing
distribution networks, took a great deal longer before the internet
existed.

An entrepreneur can now start an internet business in their bed-
room, drastically reducing the complexity and financial outlay
required to get started. Not only is it easier and cheaper than other
types of ventures, your product doesn't need to initially be perfect,

since you can always update your tools and processes later. Entrepreneurs regularly trip themselves up trying to build the perfect product before releasing it to customers. However, releasing the product to customers quickly actually accelerates the rate of product improvement. Releasing the product sooner means you can learn from your customers' feedback, using it to approach development cycles more rapidly and more iteratively. And a smaller financial outlay means that you can avoid wasting time seeking outside capital, or opt for more efficient modes of fundraising such as convertible notes.

There are a few key themes in the difference between software companies and other types of businesses, but one of the biggest takeaways is the change in perspective it causes: with software, you can spend less time trying to forecast and plan every step of the business and more time developing your business and perfecting it along the way.

This shift in thinking — i.e. the strategy of small, incremental changes, and "figuring it out along the way" — is important to the subject of this chapter. This new mindset advocates that you don't need to have everything perfectly figured out and planned before you launch your new business. It is a powerful tool in your journey as an entrepreneur. Further, there are tools available to complement this process, which we will introduce in this chapter.

4.2 The Problem with Business Plans for Startups

Before canvases, most entrepreneurs depended on a tool called the "business plan" to develop their business strategies. Business plans are sometimes (humorously) referred to as "long documents that nobody reads." The goal of this document is to tell the comprehensive story of the company including its vision, mission, product offerings, team, and more.

The language in a business plan is formal and the length often reaches 20–50 pages. This document is supposed to encapsulate all of the opportunities and risks behind this business and serves as an advertisement for future investors, partners, and team members. When business plans were more popular, it was less burdensome to ask someone to devote the time to read 20–50 pages. However, in the 2020s, this is a big "ask" and you cannot make this request to most people.

Business plans can be helpful for established businesses because these organizations have history and experience to draw from. There are all manner of data points, including financial statements and previous customers that can be used to predict future outcomes. Further, some of the more complex elements of a business plan, like extrapolation data, forecasts, and financial estimates, can be made feasibly and accurately when this historical information is available. However, when these historical data are not available, these projections are essentially guessing, and have such a high rate of error that they are minimally useful.

A startup, however, is a new entity that does not have the advantage of this prior knowledge. Most of the time, a startup is attempting to solve a problem in a new way with few resources and newly assembled teams. These attributes increase the amount of uncertainty, and this increased uncertainty is one of the reasons that startups tend not to find much value in business plans.

Writing a formal business plan is a time-consuming process. Carefully crafting the language and creating a narrative that ties the document together represents hours and days that could be better used on beneficial activities such as getting feedback from customers to improve the offering and generating leads for new prospects. As we state throughout this book, time is a highly scarce resource for entrepreneurs, and they must carefully allocate it into efforts that are most productive for the development of their venture. Frequently, business plan creation does not fit this criterion of being the most productive application of this resource.

Another argument against startups creating business plans is how rapidly conditions within these new businesses change. A startup is an organization with a lot of uncertainty, so important aspects of this business will often change: customer segments will become more specific, market demands will shift, and teams within the business will undergo changes in the organizational structure. It is not uncommon for a business plan to become outdated mere weeks after it is completed. This can occur for a variety of reasons, like discovering something from observing a competitor or finding an insight simply from executing the business. This further lowers the value of long, comprehensive business plans for customers.

4.3 The Rise of the Canvas Business Planning Format

In the 2000s, a new style of business planning tool became popular with entrepreneurs. This new approach did away with composing long prose and shifted to a more rapid, more visual style.

These tools are called canvases, which are documents that encapsulate the entirety of the venture at a high level, all in one page. A canvas is a single sheet of paper printed out that is subdivided into boxes that are to be filled in with pen or pencil. These boxes provide a structure and a framework to focus on the most crucial aspects of a new venture.

There are several types of canvases and more are evolving every day: Two of the most popular are the Lean Canvas and the Business Model Canvas (Figure 4.1). These gave rise to the Social Lean Canvas, the Value Proposition Canvas, the Creative Lean Canvas, and many more. Just like the original Lean Canvas, the adoption of these canvases will embody the same principles as the adoption of the original version: if it is solving a problem and creating value for an audience, it will catch on. We have no official stance on the ideal canvas to use: each one serves a different purpose and addresses different aspects of the business. Explore as many as you like, but we recommend starting out with the Lean Canvas (it is also the canvas that we use during the 3DS programs). The Lean Canvas is a tool to help you evaluate the strengths and weaknesses of a product or service.

The Lean Canvas was created by an entrepreneur named Ash Maurya, who is in many ways the "philosophical godfather" of 3DS. He built this tool based on frustrations he had with the first extremely popular one-page framework, the Business Model Canvas, a tool authored by an entrepreneur named Alex Osterwalder.

Business Model Canvas

Key Partners	Key Activities	Value Propositions	Customer Relationships	Customer Segments
	Key Resources		Channels	
Cost Structure		Revenue Streams		

Figure 4.1a.   The Business Model Canvas

Lean Canvas

Problems	Solutions	Unique Value Proposition	Unfair Advantage	Customer Segments
	Key Metrics		Channels	
Cost Structure		Revenue Streams		

Figure 4.1b.　Lean Canvas (bottom).

Specifically, he felt that the Business Model Canvas failed to address the risk and uncertainties inherent in the earliest stages of a startup. The Lean Canvas emphasizes simplicity: for example, "value propositions" in the Business Model Canvas condenses down to a single "unique value proposition" in the Lean Canvas.

What both canvases accomplish is to provide a focus on the most important aspects of a business. The Lean Canvas and the Business Model Canvas both place a big emphasis on customers. How do you recognize this emphasis? Look at the size of the boxes titled "Customer Segments" — the bigger the box, the more attention that topic requires. Note how this is a big deal. A business plan offers no guidance on how long each section should be, but these canvases provide visual guidance from the start.

4.4 Elements of the Canvas

Canvases put the focus first and foremost on the customers. As we stated previously, not having a defined customer base can kill a startup. Your customers can't be everyone. If your company sells shoes, it is not specific enough to say your customers are people who have feet. The customer box directs attention to the specific group of people you call your customers.

These canvases also place strong emphasis on the problem customers face (Problems even has its own large box on the Lean Canvas). This ensures that the entrepreneur focuses on solving an actual problem for likely customers. This part of the canvas returns an entrepreneur's focus to making sure that they create value for someone.

Canvases also include a box for the solution, which gives the entrepreneur a space to think about the nature of the solution they are offering and if it in fact solves a problem for the customer. These three sections of the canvas — the customer, problem, and solution — help the entrepreneur keep their attention on the areas that matter most.

The canvases also provide a framework to evaluate the operational aspects of the business. The Lean Canvas allows one to think about the financial aspects such as revenues and costs. These boxes matter because our thinking around customer, product, and solution are irrelevant if the financial fundamentals of our business idea are flawed. If a startup's revenues show no potential of ever exceedding its costs, our sustainability is in doubt, which will hurt our ability to execute on the business as well as convince others to support our efforts.

We don't calculate revenues and costs in a vacuum. If a company is massively profitable, other companies will notice and consider pursuing the same opportunity. When other companies enter the market, your revenue and cost calculations must now be understood in the context of your competitors' cost calculations. Why is this? Because customers regularly decide which product or service they will buy based on price.

Competition is important because it allows us to understand how our offering fits into the overall market landscape. Perhaps more importantly, competitors are a great source of learning.

Note: some products and services are so new or positioned so specifically that the founder will proudly declare that they have no competition. But a company always has competition in some form or fashion.

Competitors are entities that produce similar offerings that rival one another. But there are situations where another offering may not be a direct competitor but a substitute. A substitute is a product or service that can solve the same problem but in a different way, i.e. with a different technology, process, or approach to solving the problem that you address. Consider pens. Bic and Uni-ball are two of the most recognized pen brands in the world. In this case, a substitute would be a pencil company. A pencil is an entirely different product category, but can address some facets of the value proposition: a tool that can write on a surface.

The most fundamental equation in business is $P = R - C$, which is the basic expression of how a business makes money.

P = Profit
R = Revenue
C = Cost

Revenue, also known as income, refers to money that enters the business through purveying goods and services. Capital raised through investors does not constitute revenue. Revenue refers to money that comes *in.*

Money that goes out of a business is known as a cost. This term addresses money spent on sustaining the operation of the business, and can represent anything from employee salaries to inventory to web hosting. When we subtract C from R, we are left with profit. This is the money that the organization can then extract from the company or reinvest in the business.

Each company has its own P, R, and C numbers, and the relationship among them is how we evaluate the financial viability of a startup. If a company's revenues just barely exceed it's costs, while a different company is able to provide the same value with a significantly less expensive cost structure, this second company could lower it's prices to force the first one out of the market. Revenue, cost, and competitor structures matter and the Lean Canvas gives us helpful insights.

A business is not simply the customers involved and the operational components; it is also a set of people and groups involved in the creation and delivery of value to these customers. We call these other individuals "stakeholders," and they reflect the hierarchy and relationships between humans in a hierarchical structure.

Some examples of stakeholders are suppliers, channel partners, vendors, and more. These are groups your business depends on to function. For example, if your business reaches its users and customers through an iPhone app, then Apple's app store is a key stakeholder. If you deliver startup events, the venue owners who you rent the space from to host your events are partners.

Sometimes these relationships are simple. For example, many startups contract with an accountant outside of the company before they are ready to hire a bookkeeper or controller and this often happens years before they hire a Chief Financial Officer.

Sometimes these relationships are more complicated. Some companies make products referred to as "CPG." CPG stands for "consumer packaged goods" and refers to a physical product available on store shelves, typically restocked over time due to regular use. Pantyhose, glue, paper towels, and shaving cream are all examples of CPG goods. Walmart is the biggest seller of CPG goods in the United States, and their power as a stakeholder is immense. A new venture that gets access to their infrastructure and customer base receives an opportunity to reach millions of customers, which can provide a lift in sales numbers in orders of magnitude larger than previous quarters. Such wins are not always positive. Such huge volumes can cause a company's production capacity to falter and displease customers and stakeholders such as Walmart.

Walmart, then, is a vendor. They are a key distribution channel, i.e. how you reach your customers. Walmart has a massive amount of power in this relationship because they control access to customers. If your product is the best product in its category to ever exist, it doesn't mean you are guaranteed to sell them by the truckload if your customers are not aware of the product and how to obtain it. Millions of Americans go to Walmart every week; their purchasing decision is defined entirely by what is on their shelves, regardless of how easy it might be to find online options.

All vendors ask their suppliers (your company, if you are selling to Walmart) to follow what are called vendor requirements. Anytime a company sends its products to Walmart it has to arrive in a specific way: shrink-wrapped, palletized, labeled, and more all on the right day and time to the right location. If any of these variables are handled incorrectly, Walmart fines your company. Such is the price one has to pay to do business with the biggest distributor in the United States.

Note also that these issues are not constrained to in-person retail vendors. Amazon warehouses carry their own set of vendor requirements as well. And digital goods are not exempt: Apple's app store has strict requirements for receiving approval to be available to the millions of people who have access to the app store. At the time of this writing, Epic Games (the maker of Fortnite) is in a battle with Apple over pass-through payments, and the result of this conflict will settle some outstanding concerns that app store developers have with Apple's stewardship of the app store. These examples are not unique, and all stakeholders have specific considerations you must take into account when developing a business framework, and shoud be noted on a canvas you are creating for this purpose.

Now that we have addressed the content that the Lean Canvas forces you to generate, there are some noteworthy aspects of the structure of canvases also worth covering. Canvases are one page long, which is by design. This concise length has a big impact on the user experience. Completing a one page, visually organized document is far less intimidating than having to compose a double-digit lengthy prose document like a business plan. Limiting the size of the document demands that you focus on the high-level challenges and not get lost in the details.

This notion of prioritization — directing your attention and focus to the "right" things — is important as well. Time is the most limited resource an entrepreneur has and literally the one thing that is not renewable. And that is what these canvases do. They constrain your thinking around the areas that matter the most. Startups are difficult and confusing in that there is so much work to be done. But much of the work is simply not crucial in the early days. Some companies get hung up on the name of the company. Or the logo and branding. Or making sure that their vision of the prototype is perfectly executed. But the Lean Canvas directs you to what matters most. There is no box devoted to less important things like logos and branding. And the customer and problem boxes are bigger than the solution box.

Some people argue that it is perfectly acceptable that other people do not like business plans and that the thinking and effort behind composing them are where the real learning happens. In other words, it is fine that no one else reads it. We staunchly disagree. Human beings accomplish the most impact when they collaborate and a user-friendly, one-page document is significantly easier for collaboration than a business plan. Asking a mentor or advisor to comment on your Lean Canvas or Business Model Canvas is a standard practice and generates excellent discussion and analysis. Feedback is a key concept for all entrepreneurs so it makes sense to take advantage of tools that increase our ability to receive it and tighten our feedback loops.

4.5 Creating a Canvas for Your Business

Typically, it takes 30–60 minutes to complete a Lean Canvas or Business Model Canvas. The goal of completing it is not to perfectly understand every aspect of your business in detail. As stated earlier, that is simply not possible. What these canvases allow you to do is to identify and assess what you know and do not know about your business. It will help you understand strengths and weak spots of your business and your product offering.

Note that some aspects may be more or less defined than others, which is perfectly fine. Use this knowledge to guide you on how to steer the business in the future to capitalize on strengths and adjust accordingly with weaknesses. A canvas is an iterative document and is never truly "done". Often, an entrepreneur will complete a canvas several times in one sitting and dozens of times over the life of the business. At 3DS programs, teams rarely complete the Lean Canvas only once. Most complete it several times.

Iterating through a canvas quickly provides a snapshot of the business, and just like a snapshot it is quick and simple, which saves you more time to focus on other tasks in the venture.

Canvases are a truly powerful tool and we are delighted to share them with you. To learn more about canvases, check out Ash Maurya's *Running Lean* and Alex Osterwalder's *Business Model Generation*. The 3DS playbook (3daystartup.org/playbook) also contains extensive materials.

4.6 Conclusion

As technology evolves, entrepreneurs need new tools better-suited to the current business climate. Technology advances require entrepreneurs to move more quickly than previously. Whereas Business Plans — lengthy documents that fully encapsulate a worldview and a long-form strategic plan — used to be extremely valuable to the entrepreneurial journey, the internet era of business has shifted focus to canvases.

Canvases are better tools for founders because they emphasize iteration and action, as opposed to an overreliance on theory and strategy. They are visual tools that use a structure to draw focus on specific subject areas. While there are many canvases out there, the Business Model Canvas and the Lean Canvas are two of the most proven and popular. In this chapter, we have discussed the Lean Canvas in detail.

The Lean Canvas brings special attention to key elements of a fledgling enterprise: the problem that you as an entrepreneur solve, the customer segments you serve, your solution, how you measure your success, your unfair advantage and unique value proposition, as well as your revenues and costs.

Completing a Lean Canvas is a simple but essential activity for understanding the strengths and weaknesses of a business opportunity, and more importantly, steering you toward areas of focus.

References

1. https://en.wikipedia.org/wiki/Business_Model_Canvas#/media/File:Business_Model_Canvas.png.

Chapter 5

Financing Your Startup with Equity Funding

5.1 Introduction

You have probably come across equity funding at some point during your entrepreneurial journey. Equity funding is a mechanism for businesses to raise capital in exchange for a percentage of ownership in that company. This type of funding comes in various embodiments, including Venture Capital, Angel Investment, and Mezzanine Capital (sometimes referred to as Convertible Debt). It receives a disproportionate amount of attention in startup culture: Equity investors (the individuals or firms that provide capital for equity funding) are often the most sought after and difficult to connect with in a startup ecosystem. Subsequently, there are many articles that are solely written to announce when a startup receives this type of funding. Further, some startups will even name prominent equity investors in their company as part of their summary or tagline.

It is understandable why people get excited about equity investment. An individual or firm (that is possibly famous or prestigious in the world of entrepreneurship) is giving you money to grow their business. Further, unlike a loan, you don't have to pay back this investment, and it can feel like "free money" (it is not — more on this later). Further, these investors are betting that your business will be successful, and that they will make money by investing for equity. As a result, many entrepreneurs use equity funding as a source of validation for their business or even themselves personally.

However, this mindset is shortsighted, and does not comprehensively consider the benefits and drawbacks that come with equity investment. As a result, a responsible founder will go deeper when considering this investment route, and try to conduct a comprehensive analysis of whether equity funding is needed. Further, if they decide that equity funding is the best path to take, they will also consider how and when to optimally pursue this funding strategy.

In this chapter, we will NOT tell you how to seek equity investment — there are many other books and resources out there that will tell you this. Instead, we will introduce some concepts to take into account when considering pursuit of equity funding. This includes determining whether this type of funding is best for your startup (as well as some other types you might pursue). We will introduce the roles investors of this type might play in your business. We will also introduce some other funding methods that might be more appropriate for some startups. The ultimate goal of this chapter is to allow the reader to comprehensively evaluate equity funding and how it may factor into their entrepreneurial journey.

5.2 The Role of Equity Investment

Equity investment plays a specific role within the startup world. New businesses are usually very volatile, and considered too risky for traditional financing like business loans. They often do not have reliable customers or cash flow necessary to make regular loan repayments. As a result, banks are not interested in lending to these companies until they have a history of regular sales (typically 12 months or more).

To fill this gap, investors will instead invest money in a company in exchange for a portion of ownership (often referred to as "equity" or "shares"). This investment does not need to be repaid with interest like a traditional loan does. Instead, if the company grows in value, this equity will grow in value as well, producing a financial return for the investor. Equity investors take an interest in having the companies they invest in grow, as it will lead to an increase in value for the shares they own. Subsequently, they will often contribute to a company in additional ways beyond capital to help a business succeed. As a side note, employees of startups also often receive equity as part of their compensation. However, instead of contributing capital, they are contributing labor to the startup, through receiving a salary that is typically lower than the industry average for a comparable position. However, this equity gives them a piece of ownership in the company they work for, and motivates them to want the company to succeed. This equity further leads to these employees being more passionate about their job, as working to help their startup become successful leads to a financial return for them as well.

Because equity investors are investing in volatile companies, there is a significant chance their investments will lose money if the companies they invest in fail. However, if successful, they can be handsomely rewarded, sometimes to the tune of tens or hundreds of times what they put in (this often is denoted as a multiple of their initial investment: for example, "10×" means a return of 10 times what they put in, 50× means 50 times what they invested, etc.). While many of these risky bets do not produce a financial return, the investments that are successful are usually so lucrative that they cover the losses of the ones that do not produce a return. This dynamic strongly influences equity investor behavior, and they are primarily interested in startups that can successfully pursue this rapid growth and expansion.

Further, investors will only realize money from their investment when they sell their ownership stake to someone else. This is not a straightforward process, as potential purchasers are not abundant. As a result, equity investors are constantly thinking about how they might sell shares of their investments, including who they might sell these shares to, when the best time to do this might be, and other variables that will help maximize their return on investment.

The term *Exit Strategy* is used to describe different ways investors (and others that own equity in a startup) can sell their shares to others. There are a few different ways this can occur — examples include:

- Initial Public Offerings (IPO) — A business sells small parts of their company (referred to as *Shares*) on a public stock market (anyone can buy or sell shares on this market). When this occurs, the business transitions into a publicly traded company, and is bound by certain regulations that apply to all publicly traded companies (including publicly disclosing information they might not otherwise disclose).
- Acquisitions — Most or all equity for a business is bought by a single purchaser. Sometimes this purchaser is a large company that wants the startup for strategic reasons (i.e. complementing other product lines of the company). Other times, the purchaser wants to acquire intellectual property or expertise that the startup has. The purchaser can even be a competitor that doesn't want to continue competing with the startup.
- Buyouts — Someone else — often someone already involved with the business — buys equity from others.

Founders that are considering pursuing equity investment for their startups must think of the significant influence investors will have on their startup's future direction, and if it fits their vision for their business. They must consider if investors will encourage the type and rate of growth they want to pursue. Further, founders must consider what kind of exit strategy (if any) they want for their business, and if it will fit with potential investors. Later in this chapter, we will introduce some questions to consider if equity investment is a good fit.

Example: Misconceptions of Equity Funding

While equity funding gets a lot of attention and interest from media, it is not always accurately portrayed by these sources. As a result, there are some misconceptions that we frequently encounter during our entrepreneurial work. Some of the most common misconceptions about equity financing, and a more accurate way to consider these themes, are as follows.

Misconception #1: All startups need Equity Investment to be successful

A majority of new businesses do not receive equity financing (historically, this figure is less than 1%[2]). This includes many businesses that go on to be very successful. Further businesses that do receive this investment are not guaranteed to be successful either. There are many businesses that receive funding, and still go on to be commercial failures. For example, among all funded businesses, ~1% have exits at a value greater than $1 Billion (a benchmark frequently used to gauge startup success).

There is definitely some selection bias that contributes to this misconception. There are many articles that announce a company completing a funding round. Further, startups that have successful exits receive significantly more attention than those that don't. So, while it may seem like every successful startup receives equity funding, a comprehensive analysis would reveal this is not the case.

Misconception #2: Equity Investment is needed as validation for a startup

Some founders see equity investment as validation of their business idea (e.g. "If a rich person is investing in my startup, it means I am doing something right"). You will even see some startups name-drop their investors when presenting their idea to others.

It is true that having investors can serve as a form of validation, and that some people respond positively to a startup being backed by a big-name investor like Peter Thiel or Sequoia Capital. However, this should not be the only reason to pursue equity funding. Because you are giving up equity, influence, and some control of your business, it is best to use investors in a way beyond just making the founders feel good about themselves. Some ways that equity investment can help a startup is funding R&D that is otherwise not possible, helping build

(Continued)

infrastructure to scale up and grow, or utilizing an investor's network to identify and pursue important business partnerships.

Misconception #3: This type of investment is "Free Money"

When a startup receives equity funding, that money invested does not go to the founder, but instead goes into the business. The funds will be allocated for a specific purpose that is usually determined before financing is received. It is not a payday or "cashing out" like some expect it to be, and founders personally don't receive any wealth.

Further, investors will expect more than money in return for their investment. In addition to owning a percentage of the company (based on its valuation of the company and the amount they invest), they will ask for influence in startup strategy decisions. Investors will often ask for one or more seats on the board of directors, and possible other decision-making authority as well. Further, they will use this influence to push for rapid growth, and other activities that will maximize the return on their investment. As a result, it is important to consider if your investors interests align with your own and that of your startup.

Misconception #4: There are not enough Equity Investors for all startups

When we teach in various entrepreneurship ecosystems, we often hear entrepreneurs and other stakeholders complain that there are not enough funding opportunities for startups. In fact, the opposite is true, and there is more equity investment capital available than there are investment-ready startups. One explanation for this disparity is that equity investment is very focused, and only appropriate for a small set of businesses (high risk, high growth startups that can produce a large return in a specific time frame). As a result, there are many businesses that have a lot of great potential to be financially successful and create innovative products that will ultimately never receive equity funding.

A more accurate way to consider this topic is that equity investment does not serve a majority of startups. Equity investors know this, and only seek out businesses that are a good fit for their model. However, there are many other types of funding available for startups (which we will describe later in the chapter), and startups have many funding options to help grow their businesses.

5.3 The Benefits and Drawbacks of Equity Funding

Despite how it is sometimes portrayed in the media, equity investments are not only upsides. While there can be significant benefits to this form of financing, it comes with some conditions and consequences that should be considered in the decision to pursue equity funding.

As soon as a business receives equity investment, the founders stop working solely for themselves and begin working (at least partially) for someone else. Investors will come in with their own goals, thoughts, and opinions on what makes for good business strategies. Further, because they want to make money, they will often remain active in their investee to promote what they feel is the best way to grow. However, some people identify the independence to chart their own path as one of the biggest draws to entrepreneurship for them, and founders should be aware that accepting equity investment means giving up some of this independence.

Further, investors gain significant amount of influence when they invest in a company. Every equity investment comes with a *Term Sheet*, which is a set of conditions that both sides agree to. These term sheets include non-monetary conditions that are necessary criteria for an investor to provide funding. Examples of things that investors will ask for in these term sheets include a guaranteed number of seats on the startup's board of directors, the ability to approve or block significant company decisions, and sometimes even the ability to replace the Chief Executive Officer (CEO) and other key leadership.

There are many successful and productive partnerships between investors and the startups they invest in. Investors often have extensive expertise and industry connections, which they are willing to utilize to help a business they invest in grow. However, conflicts between founders and investors do occur, and can be detrimental to a business. Sometimes founders will be forced out of their own business due to disagreements with investors (a prominent example of this is when Steve Jobs was ousted from his first stint as CEO of Apple in 1985). This can be mitigated by researching potential investors extensively, and making sure that their goals align with yours. However, founders must be ready for this dynamic when considering partnerships with investors.

When a startup receives equity investment, its founders are committing to aim for it to be a high growth company. These investments are high risk, and those making the investment expect a high return if successful. Therefore, investors will push the company to pursue the rapid growth necessary to make these returns possible. Some founders would want to pursue this high rate of growth anyway, and would appreciate the push and help from investors. However, others may have a lower tolerance for the level of risk that comes with this rapid growth, or prefer a slower and less volatile approach to growing their business. Other founders might become exhausted by constantly pursuing growth. Further, growing too fast can increase the chance of a business failure. Premature scaling is frequently cited as one of the most common causes of startup failure.[3] There is no right answer to what is the best strategy, and it is based on their personal preferences. However, equity funding eliminates some options, as investors will always push the businesses they invest in to grow quickly.

Finally, fundraising takes a lot of time when done correctly. It entails many different actions including (but not limited to) determining company value and funding amount needed; making investor materials (like a pitch deck and prospectus); identifying and contacting potential investors; and preparing for the countless meetings that fundraising entails. Throughout this book, we've mentioned that time is one of the scarcest resources for founders and their new business, and this means that other actions must be postponed to dedicate time to pursue equity funding.

5.4 Questions to Determine if your Startup Should Pursue Equity Funding

When a founder is determining whether or not to pursue equity funding for their startup, there are a diverse set of considerations that should be taken into account. There is no one-size-fits-all approach to this, and it should be considered on a case-by-case basis. The following are some of the questions that you should be able to confidently answer before pursuing equity funding.

Is funding critical for my startup to advance?
There are some businesses that have little to no chance of succeeding without equity funding. These might include businesses that need capital for R&D, obtaining large equipment for manufacturing, achieving economies of scale, etc. However, this funding is by no means crucial for **every** business to advance. Many successful businesses never receive funding, and grow solely by reinvesting profits into growing the business further (referred to as *bootstrapping*, which we will elaborate on later in this chapter).

Even if funding is not critical for a business, there are still times when it is beneficial for a new business. When this is the case (i.e. when a business already has a revenue stream from paying customers), founders have greater flexibility over when they pursue equity financing, allowing them to do so on more favorable terms.

A startup should know the necessity of outside investment, as it will not only determine if it should pursue equity financing, but how and when to do so. This leads us to the next question founders should consider.

Will Equity Funding Lead to Opportunities not Otherwise Available?
When an investor or firm invests in you, they "join your team," and have a stake in your startup's success. As a result, investors will sometimes leverage other resources beyond money to help your business succeed.

If you determine that your business needs equity funding, it is important to search for an investor or firm that will give benefits beyond just providing capital. This entails a lot of internet research, talking with potential investors, and sometimes even meeting with other startups that they have invested in. Even though it can be time-consuming, you want to do extensive research into potential investors to ensure they are the best possible fit for your startup.

Am I ok with running a high-growth business?
Equity investors take a high risk by investing in new, volatile businesses. As a result, they expect a high rate of return from investments that end up being successful. Equity investors expect a high rate of growth to produce these returns (typically 10×–100× in a 3–5-year time span).

As a result, investors will always be pushing for a fast rate of growth. While some founders are not deterred and even enjoy the constant intensity that this entails, others can become exhausted by the never-ending cycle of expansion. Further, many people would be much more satisfied with a business that grows modestly (i.e. 5–10% growth annually). While media often portrays high-growth companies as more exciting and "sexy," there is no single "best" type of business — many owners of moderate growth companies find their businesses very satisfying and fulfilling. The answer to this question will be based on your personal preferences as a founder.

Is fundraising the most valuable use of time to develop your business?
Fundraising is often referred to as a "full-time job" based on the time requirement it entails. Further, it is not a straightforward or linear process. Some meetings and networking will not lead anywhere. However, you still have to consider and pursue all reasonable leads when fundraising.

As we've already stated throughout this book, founders are almost always overworked, and have to prioritize what tasks they complete for their business. When pursuing funding, this means that other actions must be put on hold to make time for fundraising. It is up to you to decide if fundraising should be a top priority, of if there are other actions you should focus on instead.

What exit strategy do I envision for my startup? Does it match the goals of investors I am pursuing?
Investors are very interested in founders and startups that envision exit strategies that will help them make money. Some founders will not be interested in selling their business anytime soon, and their exit strategy is to run a successful business for most or the entirety

of their careers. There is nothing wrong with having this goal, and many business owners take this approach. However, if this is the case, these founders should not consider equity funding, as it will likely not align with equity investor goals.

Are there other types of funding that might be better suited for my startup?
While it might be the most discussed method of funding, Equity Financing is not the only way to provide capital for a startup, nor is it the perfect match for every venture. Sometimes founders will overlook other funding types that might better complement their business based on their needs and current statuses.

Some other financing options that can work very well for a startup:

- Bootstrapping (sometimes referred to as "no financing"): This method entails reinvesting profits a business makes into growing the business further. The advantage of this method is that founders do not give up any equity or have loan repayments, and can use time that would be spent on fundraising on other actions. However, bootstrapping can often slow growth. Further, a business with especially long cash flow cycles might not be able to bootstrap effectively.

  Crowdfunding/presales: There has been a recent growth of sites like Kickstarter, or Indiegogo, where businesses can use crowdfunding for their business. This is advantageous in that startups receive funds before they have to deliver a product. Further, it removes the guesswork of how many of a product to make before delivery (inventory-constrained cash flow can be a large challenge for startups).

  Another big advantage of this method is that a business does not give up equity through this process. Further, crowdfunding campaigns can also be used to help marketing goals of the startup (some smart crowdfunding campaigns help inform likely customers of a new product or service offered). Some very savvy entrepreneurs will use crowdfunding as a form of customer validation (i.e. use presales to learn what customers are most willing to buy). As a result, there are many appealing reasons to consider crowdfunding.

However, crowdfunding does not work well for every business. It is most effective for consumer products that customers can get excited about. For example, B2B internal communication software would probably not get much interest on a crowdfunding platform. Further, your reputation can be damaged if you cannot deliver what you promise in a crowdfunding campaign.

- Grants: Sometimes grants are available for startups. One great benefit of grant funding is that the funds they provide do not have to be paid back, and they take no equity from a business. However, grants are only available for certain products and industries. Further, applying for grants takes a lot of time — applications can ask for a lot of information/materials, and there is a lot of uncertainty for funding success. Finally, the agencies that give grants — which often include government agencies — can move very slowly. Some grants require applications six months before a decision is made and any funds are given. Hence, some startups that move and change too quickly for grants are not a good match for this financing option.
- Traditional banking loans — Some startups do pursue a business loan. Typically, this requires the business to have a history of consistent or growing revenue (typically 12 months long), and the maximum amount available depends on this revenue amount. These loans do have to be paid back with interest, which can create a challenge for a new business. However, such lenders don't try to influence the direction of your startup like equity investors would.

The diverse funding options listed above should reinforce that there is no "best" financing option for your startup. Instead, you should carefully consider which one would be the optimal fit for you. Further, funding that is the best fit right now might not be the ideal choice in the future. As startups grow, their needs evolve as well, which might lead to a different financing option becoming most appropriate.

5.5 Conclusion

Equity funding is a popular and frequently discussed source of financing within the world of startups. As a result of this attention, it is sometimes seen as a milestone that all startups should strive to attain on their journey to creating a successful business. However, founders must look beyond the glamour and consider the benefits and drawbacks that come with this type of funding.

Equity financing should be seen as a single tool among many that founders can use to grow their businesses. As with all tools, you should pick the one that is most appropriate, not the most exciting (For example, a video about a screwdriver will get fewer views on YouTube than one about a hydraulic press. However, when you need to tighten the screws on a cabinet hinge, the screwdriver is a much better choice). Responsible founders must determine if equity financing is a good funding strategy through an honest and comprehensive assessment of its benefits and drawbacks for their individual ventures.

References

1. Zider, B. (1998, November-December). How Venture Capital Works. *Harvard Business Review*. Retrieved from https://hbr.org/1998/11/how-venture-capital-works.
2. Mulcahy, D. (2013, May). Six Myths About Venture Capitalists. *Harvard Business Review*. Retrieved from https://hbr.org/2013/05/six-myths-about-venture-capitalists.
3. Cook, J. (2011, September 1). The No. 1 reason startups fail: Premature scaling. *GeekWire*. Retrieved from https://www.geekwire.com/2011/number-reason-startups-fail-premature-scaling/.
4. Patel, N. (2015, April 30). How to Avoid the Premature Scaling Death Trap. *Entrepreneur*. Retrieved from https://www.entrepreneur.com/article/245603.

Part 3

Entrepreneurship Communications and Relationships

Chapter 6

Startup Pitching

6.1 Introduction: The Importance of Verbal Communication

The ability to craft and deliver a great pitch is one of the most powerful tools in an entrepreneur's toolbox. Founders will constantly be sharing infoirmation about their fledgling business, and the product or service it offers, with others in diverse formats and settings.

While the term 'pitching' can have many different meanings, in this chapter, we will define it as presenting your business to an audience to win their interest. A pitch might be to a large room containing hundreds of people. Alternatively, it could be to a single person who is an important prospect who could become your biggest customer. It might be to an investor as you all chat in a hallway at a conference. In this chapter, we will introduce some of the audiences that you will pitch to as an entrepreneur. Further, we will introduce what content goes into common types of startup pitches.

The great thing about pitching is that it is something that anyone can do. No specific skills, experience, or technical know-how is required to construct and deliver an effective pitch. Like other crucial entrepreneurship abilities (i.e. customer engagement), this skill can be learned by anyone. Further, pitching does not require large sums of capital or other resources. It's hard to build a product or hire team members without money. But creating and giving an effective pitch simply requires some effort and iterating your way to a winning message.

Pitching takes many sizes and shapes. There is no set format or process, and a good pitch can take many different forms. Some pitches walk the audience through dozens of slides in a formal environment, such as a room full of people wearing suits and business professional attire. Others are less formal and feel more like a conversation than a formal presentation. Some pitches are even given off the cuff and delivered in under thirty seconds in an elevator.

At the end of the day, the goal of a pitch is to get your audience interested enough to want to learn more about your business. As a startup founder or early stage employee, you will be pitching near constantly. If that sounds intimidating, just set those fears aside for now. Pitching, like so many things in life, gets easier and easier the more you do it.

Pitching, at its core, is about effectively communicating your startup. Telling the story of your startup in a compelling way is what will create additional opportunities. Each time you tell that story constitutes a pitch, and you will do this hundreds (maybe even thousands) of times. Committing to learning how to pitch, including overcoming fears and discomfort with giving pitches, will open doors for you and position your startup for success.

6.2 The High Variability of Pitches

One important question that you must answer when creating a pitch is "To whom will I be pitching?" You will pitch to a wide variety of people who will play different roles in helping you advance your startup concept. The content that you include in your pitch will depend on the answer to this question. Some of the various audiences you will pitch to as an entrepreneur are elaborated as follows:

- One of the most frequent audiences you will pitch to is potential customers and users of the product or service that your business offers. Given how important it is to start with the people who will use and benefit from whatever it is your business is making, you will need to frequently pitch to them with the goal of convincing them to try out your startup's offering.

- Founders will also give pitches with the goal of convincing others to join your team as a cofounder or early employee. For this audience, you will need to demonstrate the promise of your idea and why getting on board your project is the right decision for them.
- Mentors and advisors also play important roles for any startup's development. As you might imagine, many of the best mentors and advisors are in high demand, and must choose which startups they share their limited time with. A great pitch is one of the ways you can convince this audience that you are worth advising.
- Channel and strategic partners represent another audience that will require you to pitch to them at some point. These groups have access to desirable pools of customers or key technologies and convincing them to partner with you will require a pitch.
- Pitching to potential investors also occurs frequently (for many of us, this is what first comes to mind when the term "pitching" is mentioned). Investors play important roles in startup ecosystems, and they hear pitches on a near constant basis.

For each of these different audiences, you will need to adjust the content of your pitch to ensure it is suitable for that audience. Further, the duration of a pitch will vary a great deal as well. For example, a formal pitch during a meeting with equity investors will usually entail 3–5 minutes of presenting followed by Question and Answer (Q & A) sessions of varying lengths. Alternatively, meeting a potential mentor over coffee usually means you have at least the amount of time it takes for both of you to finish your cup.

The media of your pitch will also need to vary based on the audience. Sometimes a pitch will be entirely verbal, and feel like you are delivering a soliloquy. Other times you will need a well-crafted slide deck to complement your verbal presentation, conveying impressive stats and vibrant imagery to capture your audience's attention. Some pitches will require extensive supplementary materials. These materials can take the shape of backup slides in the deck for when your audience asks questions honing in on aspects of the pitch you did not have time to cover in the body of the deck. Other times, marketing materials or exhaustive financials will make sense to bring along when you deliver the pitch. What type of supplementary materials are required (if any) comes down to the type of pitch you are giving and the type of business you are pitching.

The different kinds of pitches that a founder will give while growing their startup are too numerous to cover completely. However, in this chapter, we will go into details about two of the most common types of pitches entrepreneurs give: customer pitches and investor pitches.

6.2.1 *Customer pitches*

As we've stated throughout this book, extensive and continual focus on your customers is important for any startup to create value and succeed. Subsequently, a pitch you deliver to a potential customer is one of the first and most important pitches a founder will give.

In some of the previous companies the authors have founded, we found ourselves obsessing over the company's name, logos, and branding. While this was fun to think about, the reality is that customers don't care about these things as much as many may think. Potential customers primarily care about one thing over everything else: their problems, and how to find a solution to them. As a result, many pitches to customers start out by introducing the problem they face.

What are good examples of problems that customers face? Their problem could be that a local restaurant owner has not updated her website for a decade and feels like she needs a new one. It could be that a soccer mom craves high quality coffee but wants it from a local establishment and not from a corporate franchise. It could be that a sales director's team is underperforming and he needs better sales training. All of these problems represent opportunities where pitching might be required.

After introducing the problem, pitches often go into the solution for the problem that likely customers experience. It is important to note that simply pitching a customer a new technology does not constitute addressing a problem or a solution. Customers are not interested in the best technology, but instead the best solution to the problem they face. Many companies have failed because they overemphasized an exciting technology that never adequately addressed a problem.

Consider the Segway. This product release was one of the most hyped debuts of all time, and the gyroscopic technology was certainly eye-catching. And last mile transportation is certainly a problem as cars can only get you so far in an urban environment. But the Segway was heavy, ungainly, difficult to park, and it was impossible to look cool riding it. While it solved the problem of last mile transportation, it failed to do so in a way that was adequate for consumers.

After you have presented a problem and your solution, your pitch will need to convey why your solution is superior to existing offerings. If a problem is significant, it is likely that potential customers have tried something else to solve it. These alternatives constitute competitors for your business, and who you will be competing with for customers. There are many ways to be superior to competitors. A good place to start is "better, faster, cheaper." If your offering excels on one of these fronts, you might be on the right track to creating a product customers will buy. Note that it is best to be significantly better at one of these variables than to be slightly better at all three. Further, your customers might be predisposed to one of these factors more than others. You can use the customer research actions described in Chapter 2 to determine which this might be.

It helps to be significantly better because human beings notice big improvements more readily than smaller ones. If the improvement our product provides is not big enough to notice, customers will not appreciate it enough to switch from competitors. The product could be decidedly better than anything else, but it doesn't matter if no one knows it exists.

The term "switching costs" refers to the amount of time or resources needed for implementing a new product or service. It is an important term to consider when communicating with customers. Most customers do not like to shift from a solution they are currently using unless it offers a significant benefit. Further, the more time and resources needed to switch (i.e. retraining workers, ordering new computers), the higher a switching cost will be and the more reluctant your customers are to change. You must be aware of the switching cost for customers to change to your product, and make sure that the additional value you provide is greater than these costs. Further, a pitch must convey this additional value succinctly to convince customers to try your product.

Customer pitches will often rely less on supplementary visuals and supporting materials than pitches for other audiences. Further, these materials, if applicable, will focus more on the problem/solution they face than the inner workings of your startup. The customer doesn't want all of the details of the insides of your business and how your business model works. They want to feel like you can solve their problems and you are credible enough to be successful in the long run.

Why do they care about your startup having a long life? Because it would be inconvenient (and in some cases, disastrous) for them to take the risk of onboarding you and integrating you into their business processes only for you to disappear. This could cause service outages or bad end user experiences or any other category of problems. The larger business community is aware of the risks and short lifespans of most startups and, if they work with you, they have exposure to these risks. This is why so many early customers of a startup tend to arise from a personal connection where trust in the relationship already exists.

Lastly, customer pitches are typically quite short, and rarely run longer than five minutes. Customers usually have a strong understanding of their own needs, and don't require lots of education to understand industry problems. If your offering uses new and innovative technologies, it could take longer to explain these innovations to them.

6.2.2 *Investor pitch*

Investor pitches are another common type of pitch that founders give. These pitches are an important component of the startup process and provide great opportunities for profound insights about your business and its potential for success.

The goal of an investor pitch is to convince your audience (made up of one or more potential investors) that your business concept has a high likelihood of becoming profitable and scalable. Investors care most about receiving a return on their investment, and they seek opportunities that maximize this outcome.

Note that we did not say they invest in technologies they find cool or markets they find interesting. Also note that while your startup means everything to you, you are one of many companies in which they have invested and it is helpful to consider your relationship with them in that there likely are ten other startups who they are hoping generate outsized returns. Finally, note that they can be excellent supporters and you can develop collegial relationships, but at the end of the day their return on investment is far and away their greatest concern.

A pitch to potential investors usually takes place at their offices or a meeting place of their choosing. Always arrive early and double and triple check that your computer is charged and you have the right adapters and equipment to display your presentation.

A typical investor pitch covers the topics that allow an investor to evaluate a business concept, the upside possibilities of that concept, and the team who is executing that concept. Some common topics included in an investor pitch are as follows:

- Problem: the problem you solve for customers
- Solution: how your solution solves that problem
- Market size: the number of customers and users who experience this problem and pay for a solution. Market size is usually expressed in dollar size
- Go-to-market strategy: the plan for how to introduce this solution to the market and achieve initial growth

- Revenue model: how the business makes money
- Milestones: Significant accomplishments that you and your team have completed thus far
- Competitors: who else is trying to solve this problem for customers and your company's position in relation to theirs
- Team: the group you have assembled to take on this challenge and why your team has the skills necessary to make your business successful
- "The Ask": What you are requesting from your audience. This can be seed capital, introductions to big customers, partnership opportunities, etc.

The order in which you present these topics is not particularly important, and there is no one-size-fits-all template for the pitch or its supporting materials. However, your pitch should present a clear message with logical transitions between topics so that you can keep the attention of your audience. Were your pitch to be a checklist of tasks with no semblance of story or narrative, your audience would likely become bored and stop paying attention.

Several decades ago, investors gave a startup 40 minutes to an hour to give an investment pitch. However, the global startup boom of the last ten years has led to more entrepreneurs pursuing startups and more startups. Subsequently, investors have to be choosy about which ones they want to hear from. Today, an entrepreneur typically has about five minutes to make the presentation and, if things go well, 15–30 minutes for in-depth Q & A sessions. However, this means that one of the biggest challenges for creating an investor pitch is determining the most important 5 minutes of material to include in a pitch.

6.3 Considerations for All Pitches

The best way to create a solid pitch is to figure out what you want to say, build your slides, and practice your delivery again and again. Further, you want to make sure that your pitch will be understood by an audience with no prior knowledge of your startup. You have spent dozens (or more) hours with your startup idea and have gained extreme familiarity and details for all elements of this concept. However, your audience will not have this knowledge. Certain terms and concepts that seem second nature to you might be overly technical or industry-specific, and you must ensure that your pitch does not overwhelm your audience with information.

It is crucial that you practice your pitch multiple times, including practice in front of others so you can receive feedback. The feedback is one of the most important practices for developing a compelling pitch. Getting feedback will allow you to tweak and refine your pitch and any supporting materials, so that when you are ready to present it to potential investors, it comes off as strong and compelling.

After you give your pitch, there is usually a Q & A session where you answer questions from your audience. In some ways, this session can be as or more important than the pitch itself. This is because you have had plenty of time to make your pitch excellent and well structured. Fielding questions provides an opportunity to show investors how well you think on your feet. This is important: smart investors know that you can't foresee every problem and that business is messy and improvisational at times. They are less interested in knowing that you have all the answers; they want to know that they can count on you to find them eventually.

Therefore, in addition to practicing the formal pitch itself, it is a good idea to prepare for the Q & A session as well. Entrepreneurs will often spend a considerable amount of time preparing backup slides, which are not presented during the formal presentation, but are used to provide additional information for questions that might be asked. And as backup slides are not used in the body of a presentation, you place them at the end of the deck in case you receive a question around a topic you are knowledgeable on but which was not central enough to put in the body of the slide deck. One of the most common topics elaborated on backup slides is legal/regulatory concerns. If your startup will require some specific strategy around legal or regulatory issues, a backup slide is a good opportunity to show your initial thinking on this topic.

Even if the audience appears unimpressed with the answers on your backup slides, the fact that you have anticipated the question, and have a succinct response prepared, will reflect well on you, as it demonstrates that you anticipate challenges.

Some other tips on how to effectively handle the Q & A section of a business pitch:

- Answer questions confidently, but don't make up an answer if you don't know. Saying "I don't know yet" shows a lot of maturity as a founder, as it demonstrates that you are not claiming to know everything.

- Answer questions briefly: concise answers allow more time to hear additional questions, which represent valuable feedback. If your audience wants to know more information than you initially provide, they can always ask a follow up questions to explore the topic more deeply.

- Keep track of questions you receive: consistent questions on a single topic suggest that a point could be made in a clearer fashion, could be made into a backup slide, or could even become part of the main body of slides. You can always improve your pitch for the future, even if you have already given it.

- If the room gets quiet because the investors are thinking, resist the urge to fill the silence. Give them time to assemble their thoughts.

For all types of pitches, time is a limited resource, and you must be aware of how long you will have your audience's attention. You will never have enough time to cover all the details you would like to during the pitch. Further, it is impossible for your audience to understand your venture as comprehensively as you do. However, this is not as large a problem as you may expect. If you give your pitch effectively, your audience will remain interested, and ask questions that will allow you to expand on your startup further. The goal of a pitch is not to give them a perfect understanding of every detail of your business concept; it is to keep them interested so they will want to engage you further.

As mentioned earlier, you have had weeks and months to develop an intimate understanding of the details behind your venture. Your audience does not have that luxury. You will need to simplify several elements because too much information will overwhelm your audience. Which means that much of crafting a good pitch comes down to what you choose to leave out. What parts will generate interest and captivate the right audience? The answer to this question matters, and it is best developed by getting feedback as much as possible.

6.4 Conclusion

Pitching is a crucial skill for early stage entrepreneurs and a helpful skill for non-entrepreneurs. The need for compelling storytelling and articulating one's ideas is a key part of moving any idea forward. Know that the context and content of your pitches will vary over time, and the ability to adjust and adapt your pitch to the situation is important. Note also that the goal of a pitch is not necessarily to impart perfect understanding of your startup — the goal of a pitch is to engage your audience, so that conversations can continue to explore the finer details of your venture.

While you will pitch to all manner of audiences, customer and investor pitches tend to be the most important and the most common. A good customer pitch invites trust in the product, displays an understanding of the problem, and mitigates risk around an established company engaging a fledgling startup. An investor pitch emphasizes the market size and potential financial upside of strong performance in said market, along with presenting a strong team appropriately built out to capture such an opportunity.

In order to develop a pitch suitable for any audience, you should practice your pitch until it becomes almost instinctual and improve the content and delivery based on feedback you receive during practice. Prepping the pitch itself and how you will respond to common questions puts you in the best possible position to capitalize on opportunities to present your startup, capture the attention of your audience, and ultimately build a successful company.

Chapter 7

Mentorship

7.1 Introduction

Chapter 1 tells the story of the challenges you might face as an entrepreneur (in case you forgot: there are many!). It's hard partially because there are so many unknowns and complex situations that seem unwieldy and difficult to navigate. However, there is a category of people whose role is to help you along your entrepreneurial journey. These people are called mentors, and almost every famous entrepreneur you have heard of can point back to a mentor playing an instrumental part in their success (you might have even come across news articles where they mention their mentors as well[1]).

Mentors are the people who can guide you along your entrepreneurial journey by sharing their experience and the wisdom they gained treading a similar path. In this chapter, we define a mentor as someone who helps an entrepreneur, typically in an informal way. It is most often done on a volunteer basis, and is not as part of a formal relationship, i.e. you are not paying them, and they never carry the formal title of "Mentor".

Mentors are not the only individuals that will give advice to entrepreneurs. Investors will also give lots of advice to the startups they invest in. However, they do so because they have a financial interest in seeing their investees succeed (And sometimes, as we mention in Chapter 5, investor interests can diverge from those of entrepreneurs). Advisors also provide advice to entrepreneurs.

However, advisors often provide advice in exchange for a fee (most often in the form of a minor percentage of the company). Mentors help entrepreneurs for a number of reasons, but personal financial gain is typically not one of them.

In this chapter, we will give an overview of mentorship and the form that mentor/mentee relationships take. We will also provide some general strategies for communicating with mentors, and how to process the advice that they give you. While the mentor/mentee relationship is often informal and unstructured, its importance to founders should not be underappreciated as it can be quite pivotal to a founder's success.

7.2 The Mentor/Mentee Relationship

A common question that many entrepreneurs ask is "Who is a mentor and why do they play this role?" Mentors are typically entrepreneurs or business people in their local community who have previously attained a certain level of success in business. They are often motivated by a desire to give back — they previously benefited from access and exposure to their community and seek an opportunity to contribute to the same community that previously supported them. Often times, individuals serve as mentors because it gives them a sense of legacy. They take pride in contributing to the next generation of entrepreneurs and knowing that their time and effort are spent in the service of positive impact.

Mentors are almost always older than you (they are frequently 5–10 years older than you, though this age gap can vary a great deal). They also have achieved some success in business, and have a depth of experience from creating a startup of their own. They share this experience with their mentees, in order to leverage it to help other startups. (On a separate note, "peer mentorship" is the term used for guidance from people around the same age or level of progress as you. Getting outside feedback from peers can be a powerful learning force as well, and we have received great input from people our own age. However, mentorship from people who have "been there before" tends to be superior, and we will focus on that in this chapter).

The mentor–mentee relationship is one that we will now introduce in more depth. Mentors provide their guidance to individuals, and not the startup as a whole. Mentor relationships pertain to a mentor connecting to another person, not to an organization. The reason this is so is because human beings are social animals; we bond with individuals, and despite how much we trust a brand or an organization, we tend to derive more value from relationships with people. Note that there are other structures that give overarching advice to the company. For example, a startup's Board of Directors will give company-level advice. A startup's investors and advisors will perform this role as well.

Another question we often hear is "How many mentors can a single person have?" There is no standard number. Some entrepreneurs successfully manage 10 or more relationships. Others have a single person who they go to for advice. As a result, rather than strategize about how to obtain an "ideal" number, you should focus on developing your venture, and assess if your mentors currently address your needs as you develop your company. One common occurrence for entrepreneurs is to have specific mentors you seek out for specific types of advice (i.e. some mentors have expertise in fundraising and others have expertise in prototyping). Further, just like there is no set number of mentors a person should have, there is no consistent "depth" of the relationship you will have with your mentors. However, one thing to note is that "more" is not always "better" when it comes to mentors (we elaborate on this in the "Mentor Whiplash" section that follows). Developing a few, high-quality mentor relationships can be more beneficial than many superficial ones.

As an analogous example, consider your circle of friends. You will be closer to some friends than others, and you will likely interact with your closer friends more often. You will also be more trusting of your closer friends, and more willing to share sensitive information with them. Further, you interact with your friends in different ways — some might be those you play sports with, while others are friends from parenting and other family relationships. Mentors can be similar, and the interactions you have with them will vary greatly.

How often you communicate with your mentors will depend on the situation and the issues you are facing as an entrepreneur. Sometimes communication will be infrequent — you might contact a mentor only once or twice a year (and even then, the communication is done by email. Other times, you might be speaking with a mentor multiple times a week if you are approaching a significant milestone that aligns with their area of expertise. However much you communicate with your mentors is fine, given that you are not asking too much of them. Given the nature of mentor relationships (reminder: mentors are unpaid and typically provide mentorship out of a desire to give back to their entrepreneurship community), you want to ensure you are not overburdening your mentors with requests. Respect their time and energy by not asking too many questions or asking for too much of their time. Limit yourself to questions for which it is difficult to find answers anywhere else (i.e. don't ask them things you could learn yourself from Google research). If you are unsure if you are asking too much of them, just ask your mentor outright. They will tell you if you are overstepping your bounds.

Further, you want to be respectful of your mentors when you do meet with them. Fortunately, there are simple ways to do this. Show up on time — if not early — for any in-person meetings. Make yourself easy to find at the coffee shop or meeting venue so they do not have to wander too much to find you. Better yet, email or text them to let you know where they are. Give them the good chair — the one that is further from the bathroom or the draft coming in from the door to the outside. If it's not in person, be present for all calls. Make sure your technology — your microphones, headset, computers etc., — are all working ahead of time so that the meeting proceeds smoothly. After the session, send follow up emails thanking them for their time. Even better, recap the discussion and your next steps.

Perhaps the most important thing you can do to show appreciation to your mentors is to do what you say you will do. Let's say you present your mentor with questions about how to contact a potential customer and your mentor gives you a step-by-step way to accomplish this goal. You agree that this approach makes sense and think it is the right thing to do. If you meet with your mentor weeks or months later and you have not made any progress towards this goal, your mentor will question if spending time on you is worthwhile. Remember, many mentors are motivated by giving back to other entrepreneurs. You want to show them that their advice is creating an impact, and demonstrate that their advice is meaningful to you.

7.3 Communicating with Mentors

Another important part of managing mentor relationships is being intentional about how you ask for help. It is difficult for a mentor to help when you ask them broad, open-ended questions without context (i.e. "how do we get customers?"). A mentor can provide guidance much more easily if you explain: (a) an overview of your current status and challenges, (b) guesses you may have at why previous efforts have failed or succeeded [reasons], and (c) some potential next approaches that you are considering. In addition to making it easier on your mentors, this will also greatly increase the quality of advice you receive. Every startup is different, and the best way to approach a challenge will vary greatly from venture to venture based on specific conditions. By providing context to the current situation you are facing, they will be able to provide tailored advice that is more applicable and valuable to you.

The ideal way of framing a question is to be concise and provide the mentor with the necessary facts and context. This approach gives the mentor something to work with. Most mentors (actually, almost everyone in the advice-giving world) hate hearing "Can I pick your brain?".

To a mentor, this request feels like a preview to a rambling conversation where vague questions will be poorly posed and one's time will not be respected. This question feels lazy, as if the founder has completed the bare minimum of effort leading up to it. Unless "Can I pick your brain" is followed by, "about [specific challenge] and whether or not [option a] or [option b] makes sense for us," the question will likely frustrate the mentor.

Even if the situation where you find yourself and your company seems messy and murky, making some effort in advance to present your situation as clearly as possible to the mentor will make it easier for them to help you.

Bad Framing	Good Framing
"How do you know if you should raise investor capital?"	"We're wondering if we should try to raise money. We are at a bit of a standstill. We do not have a software developer on the team so we don't have a product. If we raise capital, would that allow us to hire software engineers?"

The most likely answer to the above question is "no." If you are a young founder, very few investors believe that you know your market well enough to build the right thing. They will want to know that you have performed proper research on your customers and they would rather you display some resourcefulness by learning how to code yourself or finding someone who will help you for free. Good framing of the question means that they can answer your question more easily and efficiently, giving you time to explore other challenges and issues.

7.3.1 *Mentor whiplash*

Earlier in the chapter, we discussed the ideal number of mentors. While almost all mentors are beneficial, it is possible to sometimes have too many. This situation often arises when you are participating in some sort of structured entrepreneurship program such as a class or an accelerator. Some of these involve "mentor speed dating" style interactions where you encounter several mentors in a short amount of time. These mentors likely have different takes on your current opportunities and challenges. Some mentors will encourage you to zig while others will tell you to zag.

This phenomenon is called "mentor whiplash" because the advice of various mentors will direct you to pursue different (sometimes contradictory) courses of action. Further, there is no single right answer, and many potential courses of action seem like they could be correct. It is important that entrepreneurs be aware of this phenomenon, and are confident to make the final decision about what they think is best for their startup. As a founder, you will know your startup better than anyone else, and are best able to decide the optimal direction for its continued development and growth.

In the early days of creating entrepreneurship programs, this would come up often for the 3DS organization, and we used to worry about the negative effects mentor whiplash could have on entrepreneurs. The avalanche of advice coming from mentors would leave participants frantically scribbling down notes of actions to take later, before going on to speak to another mentor who would suggest a completely different strategy. The entrepreneurs would sometimes get that deer-in-headlights look, confused at how to digest all of these inputs. We considered trying to find a way to erase this confusion, but realized that this would actually be a disservice to those we were trying to teach.

The ability to make a decision is an important skill for all entrepreneurs to have. In many ways, running a company is about making decisions. Good founders are decisive and make decisions early: that way, when they inevitably make an incorrect one, they have time to adjust and improve things. Less effective founders put off making difficult decisions (or look to others to make decisions for them). When the inevitable mistake does occur, there are limited other options to try other approaches or less resources are available.

As a founder, learning how to be decisive is a powerful skill. Going through the gauntlet of rapid feedback from several different mentors provides a great opportunity to acquire and hone this skill.

Regarding these mentors: they are smart people. They love giving advice. They sound so confident! They sound so sure of themselves! Just because they sound that way doesn't actually mean they know the best course of action. Further, even when you provide them extensive context and information about your startup, they will not have as much knowledge about your startup as you do. Their advice is delivered through their own lens, which may not be a good fit for you. More so, they do not have any skin in the game. If they were the founders and the decisions had implications for their lives, they might approach these situations differently.

As you grow as an entrepreneur, you learn that even the best mentors don't have all of the right answers. No one does (and frequently, there is no single "right" answer — just a set of options that are relatively better or worse than one another). However, you must make a decision and pursue it, even if you are not 100% confident about it.

Sometimes, entrepreneurs become worried if they don't end up following the advice of their mentors. They might feel as if going in a different direction will offend their mentor, or damage your relationship with them. However, a good mentor will understand that you are doing what is best for your startup, and still be interested in advising you. Further, if this situation occurs, you can explain to them why you chose to go in a different direction. The advice will still be valuable to you, and might help you out in the future. If you communicate this to your mentors, you will show they still have an impact on you, even when you don't follow their exact advice.

7.4 Finding Mentors

So how do you find a mentor? There are many different avenues.

Most mentor relationships begin from one's pre-existing personal network. Think of who you might know who might have insights or connections useful to your venture. If no one springs to mind, search various social networks to review your existing contacts: LinkedIn, Facebook, Twitter, or Instagram can reveal that you are connected to someone you forgot about. In Chapter 8, we will introduce ways you can build a professional network, and many of these practices can be applied to finding mentors as well.

If your network fails to surface anyone relevant, consider institutions to which you are connected: the school you have attended, or more directly, a startup program such as an accelerator, incubator, or meetup group in your area. Startup programs regularly connect entrepreneurs and mentors — it's a major part of their work — so they are a solid place to start.

One final concept to note when searching for mentors: Most mentor–mentee relationships don't start with the question "Will you be my mentor?" Instead, these relationships usually develop organically, after both parties know each other a bit. Earlier in the chapter we mentioned that a social connection was an important part of the mentor/mentee relationship. Asking someone to commit to being a mentor before that connection occurs is premature, and decreases the chance of a mentor agreeing to work with you. Instead, consider asking them to meet once, and see what results from that initial meeting.

7.5 Conclusion

Mentors provide valuable advice to founders, usually out of a sense of altruism. This advice comes from their experience from previous professional success. Unlike other stakeholders in an entrepreneurship ecosystem (i.e. investors), the role they play can vary highly — their advice can span a large range of topics, and mentors can come from all sorts of backgrounds. While their advice usually comes in informal and unstructured settings, the value of high-quality mentorship should not be underestimated.

While mentor advice can be highly valuable, it is not meant to be followed precisely no matter what. Mentor advice can be incomplete, confusing, and sometimes contradictory to advice from others. As the founder, you will know your startup better than anyone else, and will be the best person to decide on what course of action to take. Subsequently, it is important for founders to be decisive. Being able to choose among multiple possible courses of action is an action that founders must follow consistently when building their business, and you should not be daunted by the prospect.

Reference

1. https://www.forbes.com/sites/womensmedia/2019/12/31/the-value-of-mentorship-in-running-a-successful-business/?sh=736ee23d79bd

Chapter 8

Building a Professional Network for Startup Development

8.1 Introduction: Why a Professional Network is Important for Entrepreneurs

Entrepreneurs do not operate independent of their surroundings. They are often interacting with individuals and entities outside of their venture for a variety of reasons. Sometimes, they need to acquire personnel that have the skillset or expertise that they do not possess (as an employee or a contractor). Other times, they need advice from experienced mentors or business owners. These personnel can also lead to sales channels, partnerships, and customers that they wouldn't be able to attain on their own. The individuals that entrepreneurs are connected with can have a strong positive influence on the development of their business.

Subsequently, entrepreneurs should constantly be building and expanding their professional network (this is actually true for ALL career fields, but in this book, we are focused primarily on entrepreneurship). Further, these actions don't start after founding your business, but should be done continually at all times. As a student, one effective way to build a professional network is to be active in your classes and extracurricular activities. This will get you interacting with other students and professors, and building relationships that will help you beyond graduation. As an employee for a large company, this can entail interacting with coworkers and others in the industry where you might eventually start your business. These connections can turn into future mentors, business partners, employees for your business, and sources of support that will be critical to future entrepreneurial success.

However, these actions by themselves are not enough, and entrepreneurs should also actively be pursuing new connections with those outside of their immediate surroundings. This can be a bit trickier, as you won't just encounter these connections during their daily routine, and often have to initiate these meetings. However, there is no secret technique or skill for successful networking, and everyone is able to intentionally build their professional network regardless of educational background or professional experience.

In this chapter, we are going to introduce some general strategies and tips for building a professional network for entrepreneurship. We will discuss different ways to research, identify, and pursue contacts for a professional network. We will also discuss how to prepare for networking actions, and how to develop ongoing professional relationships. Finally, we will discuss how to set reasonable expectations for network building actions.

8.2 Actions to Grow a Professional Network

At all 3 Day Startup (3DS) programs, we have mentors come to help guide the experiential learning process. These mentors are a great addition to these programs, and many participants continue to receive advice from these mentors even after program completion. Unfortunately, this is not a common occurrence outside of 3DS programs — the mentors will rarely come to you (sorry). You have to be proactive and take intentional actions to grow a professional network.

There is no single approach to successfully growing a professional network. Effective entrepreneurs will usually employ multiple methods to build and maintain their professional network. However, many actions fall into one of two categories: directed or nondirected. A good analogy for comparing these strategies is fishing.

Directed networking is like fishing with a spear: you have to identify the fish you most want to eat, aim your spear, and hope it hits this single target. General networking is like fishing with a net — you throw the net over a wide area, and see what is caught when you pull it in. You might catch a variety of types of fish: some might not taste very good, while others might — you have less overall certainty about what you might encounter. However, by attempting to catch multiple fish at once, you increase the chance of catching something tasty.

8.2.1 *General networking (i.e. fishing with a net)*

The first approach to growing a professional network is to aim to meet as many people as possible. This can be useful for people early in their career, or those who have not spent much time previously building a professional network. This can also be a productive approach if one currently does not have a specific networking need or goal — this approach can be employed to meet others that may be helpful at a later time. Once a need arises in the future, you can call on these people to help with specific entrepreneurial goals.

8.2.1.1 *Mixers and networking sessions*

Mixers and networking sessions are events that have limited structure, which encourage attendees to discuss topics of their choosing, in order to pursue those most beneficial to them. Many in entrepreneurship recognize the importance of developing a personal network as well, so entrepreneurship-themed networking meetings are increasingly common. Networking sessions are great for meeting many people quickly (you can have 5–6 meaningful conversations in an hour), so that you can identify those you want to speak with further, and follow up without making a cold call.

Sites like Meetup.com and f6s will allow you to quickly search for events that can have beneficial networking value. Further, many of these sessions are free to attend, though you might have to sign up in advance to reserve a spot. When searching for networking sessions, consider which ones have the highest potential for encountering potential networking opportunities. You will not have time to attend every session, and you should prioritize the ones that will be most beneficial.

When you attend these networking sessions, it's important to have appropriate expectations for the depth of discussion at these functions. Do not expect to have long discussions that dive directly into highly complex topics and advice. Instead, expect many short, preliminary discussions with a range of people. The aim at these sessions is to meet a lot of people briefly, and identify those you will follow up with later.

8.2.1.2 Volunteer for events or conferences

For almost every profession and industry, there is likely a nonprofit or other organization that could utilize those skills effectively. There groups will sometimes put out calls for volunteers to help these organization's projects. In addition to being personally fulfilling, these actions can be a great opportunity to network within a certain field. The time you spend with these organizations will have you interacting with other professionals. This volunteering doesn't have to be for a charity or nonprofit either — there are many professional associations or industry groups that have similar calls for volunteers.

Meeting people during volunteering actions is similar to those you encounter at general networking sessions. Do not expect to have deep, meaningful conversations the first time you meet someone, and not everyone that you meet will become a crucial part of your professional network. Instead, a beneficial relationship will grow slowly over time, and the initial meeting can serve as the foundation for these relationships.

8.2.1.3 Building off conversations from general networking actions

Many people make the mistake of going to a networking event, having brief conversations with multiple potential beneficial contacts, and not following up on these conversations. If you do this, most of the potential value of these sessions will be lost. Conversations at these sessions tend to be brief and general, and you won't be able to focus on specific topics. Further, because most attendees are meeting many people in a short time period, they tend to forget, or blend conversations from multiple people together. Subsequently, it is in your best interest to follow up with contacts promptly. If you would like to continue the conversation that you had, you can message them asking to set up a one-on-one meeting, where you can discuss a topic in a deeper, more focused manner. However, you might also recognize that someone you met is a great potential contact, although there isn't anything to discuss currently. In this case, you can send a message thanking them for the initial conversation, and hoping you can chat with them more in the future. This will increase the chances that someone will remember you, and will be more likely to respond when you reach out to them in the future.

While there is no single way to follow up with contacts, consider what the authors do in this situation: Within 24 hours of attending a networking meeting, we try to make a list of everyone we met at the session that we would like to follow up with. This will not be everyone that we spoke to, but instead be a few that stand out as being the most helpful to future professional pursuits (for example, if you talk to 12 people at a networking session, 1–3 might be prime candidates you will want to follow up with). Within 24 hours after that, we will send a quick email or note asking to follow up. When you do make a connection, it is important to follow up promptly — people are more likely to forget who you are as time goes on. Later in this chapter, we will describe the difference between warm calls and cold calls, and why it is much better to follow up with someone familiar to you.

8.2.2 *Directed networking (i.e. fishing with a spear)*

As an alternative to general networking, it is sometimes beneficial to only reach out to specific people that will be helpful for a certain issue. Some startups need a specific type of help or expertise, and anything outside that area would not be beneficial at the time.

Alternatively, some entrepreneurs don't have the energy to continually be meeting new people, and instead prefer to save their energy for contacts they know will be valuable. Another method of networking that might stand out in these circumstances would be a directed approach, where you research and identify key contacts, and then reach out to them exclusively.

It does take some effort to identify those you want to reach out to directly, and this research can take a significant amount of time. However, directed networking typically produces fewer low utility contacts than general networking does. Further, this approach requires less time conversing with others than general networking does. Subsequently, this approach is sometimes appealing to more introverted entrepreneurs.

8.2.2.1 *Identifying potential contacts*

The first step for this networking approach is to identify potential contacts you might want to reach out to. Identifying these contacts can take significant effort, and the amount of time required for this action should not be underestimated. However, effort put into this step will ensure you identify good potential contacts, and likely increase the chance of a positive addition to your professional network.

One great place to start for this endeavor is your existing professional network. You can ask your contacts about potential names that might be beneficial for your current challenge. Like you, your colleagues will have a professional network of their own, and might have a contact they would be willing to tell you about.

Internet research is another great way to identify potential contacts for directed networking actions. This could entail using social or professional networking sites (like LinkedIn, AngelList, etc.), which might allow you to search by specific parameters like location or industry. It could also entail Google searches for specific skills or contacts in your area. Regardless of what you need, it is likely that a potential contact exists, and the real challenge is sorting through massive available information to identify them.

8.2.2.2 *Reaching out to potential contacts*

Once you have identified someone that you want to add to meet, you must figure out how to reach out to them. There are different approaches to reaching out to these people, outlined as follows. These approaches will vary highly based on familiarity with the person you are contacting, and whether there is a mutual connection.

Direct Introduction

One of the best ways to approach someone is to have a mutual contact make an introduction. This can be as simple as a quick message or email introducing the two of you, with the initial contact coming from the mutual contact. This is because people are much more likely to respond to someone they have previously known than to an unfamiliar name. Further, when someone introduces you, they are tacitly endorsing you, and implying that you are someone worth meeting. This makes an introduction one of the most powerful approaches to utilize when it is possible to do so.

LinkedIn is a great tool for identifying potential introducers, as it can show you all mutual connections (aka people that can make an introduction for you) when you look up a profile. You can also ask friends and colleagues the best way to approach someone. Don't be afraid to do some research for this step, as you may identify an approach you hadn't considered previously.

One thing to keep in mind is that when a person makes an introduction for you, they are putting a bit of their reputation on the line to help you out. If you flake out on following up with someone, it will make them look bad, and potentially damage the relationship between the two of you. Further, asking for an introduction is a fairly significant request for many people. If you ask someone to make an introduction, be ready to help them out when you can in the future. Finally, be sure not to overuse asking for these introductions — try to consider if it is important enough to ask, or if you should instead wait for a more important contact to be introduced to.

Warm Calling

Earlier in this chapter, we described some situations where you might meet someone briefly, who you would want to follow up with in the future. Sometimes you don't have time to discuss everything you want to during a brief conversation. Other times, your initial discussion leaves you with the impression that you definitely want to maintain contact with someone. Subsequently, when building your professional network, you will often find yourself contacting someone after an initial meeting (sometimes referred to as "warm calling").

As with direct introductions, warm calling takes advantage of the fact that people are much more likely to respond to someone they know than to someone that they don't. As a result, when contacting someone with this approach, it is a good idea to reference your initial meeting or conversation.

At 3DS programs, we will often meet great mentors, participants, and entrepreneurship faculty that we will want to talk to at length. However, these programs are intense, and there will not be much time to converse. As a result, we frequently find ourselves wanting to have a follow-up conversation with the great people that we meet. The example email on the following page is one we have used previously to contact these people and attempt to continue our initial conversations.

A good rule of thumb for warm contacting someone is that it is better to contact them sooner rather than later. Even if you had a great initial connection or conversation, it will become less memorable as time passes. Subsequently, contacting sooner will increase the chance of a response.

Cold Calling

If you identify someone that you want to contact, but have no connection to them, you can try "cold-calling" them, or reaching out to them with no previous interaction. This has a much lower success rate than the methods mentioned above — people get a lot of daily

Email Body	Commentary (related to underlined text)
Dear <Contact>, We met recently at the 3DS Austin program. I enjoyed our conversation during the weekend as well as your suggestions for actions on <TOPIC>. As I continue to develop my business further, I have been able to utilize this advice. However, I am running into some additional questions about TOPIC.	Remind them of where you met, and what was discussed. Brief details like this can serve as a reminder, and increase the chance of getting a reply.
Is there a time I could buy you a cup of coffee and discuss it further? You gave some great suggestions during the 3DS weekend, and I'm confident you would have other good advice to build on this conversation. I'm sure your schedule is very busy, but I would greatly benefit from any time you can share, even if just 15–20 minutes.	Introduces the "Ask", and what you are trying to get out of a meeting.
Further, I'd be happy to meet you at any time and location that would be convenient for you. With much appreciation, NAME	Be flexible, and give lots of options to meet up (they are doing you a favor).

calls and emails, and might filter your message out as spam or other junk/unimportant email. This further reinforces why it is important to have a robust personal network — as you know more people, it increases the chance you will find a mutual contact that can make an introduction for you.

The email template on the following page is an example of how one can cold-email someone that they want to meet with.

It is important to customize the emails you create for the person you are contacting. Remember, you are emailing someone who probably has no idea who you are — you want them to feel like your message is specifically for them and not a template sent out to multiple people (which they are much less likely to read). Anything that increases the chance of them reading the letter will help the likelihood of success when reaching out through cold calling. Additionally, when crafting your hook and introduction,

Email Body	Commentary (related to underlined text)
Dear NAME: As a fellow SCHOOL STUDENT/ GRADUATE, I am writing you to help me with a challenge I am currently facing. Through my coursework and past job/intern-ships, I find that I have a strong interest in FIELD.	This is the hook. This is how you attempt to connect with who you are writing with, and make them want to meet with you. You can try school connection (if you attended the same institution), field, or something else. This should go first, as they otherwise might not read the rest of the email.
Upon graduation, I am increasingly confident that I would like to pur-sue a career in FIELD. However, being relatively new to this, I am encountering some difficulty learning SKILL based on my cur-rent major and coursework.	Explains your interest. This should be in line with the person you are reaching out to.
What am I contacting you for? I have heard from a variety of trustworthy sources that you have extensive expertise in this area. I would appreciate any suggestions you might have for a recent graduate in this indus-try. Is there a time we can meet to discuss it further?	This section outlines your objective and why you want to meet with them. Sometimes it helps to be complementary (but not over the top).

(Continued)

Email Body	Commentary (related to underlined text)
I have attached a resume to demonstrate my exposure to entrepreneurship.	This is not necessary, but it can help you introduce yourself (and impress them if you have a good resume). Remember, this person has no idea who you are, and a resume helps fill in that picture.
Any help you can provide to an aspiring entrepreneur who knows the path she wants to take but needs some assistance to get started would be most appreciated. I can be readily available to meet online or in person based on what is most convenient for you. Thank you for any guidance you can provide. With appreciation, NAME	Ask nicely to meet with them. Be open to phone/Skype/other methods of contact to be accommodating. Make sure you don't sound like you are expecting anything from them.

make sure to put some thought and research into who you are reaching out to, and customize this text accordingly. Cold calling can be challenging, and you want to do anything you can to maximize the chance of receiving a response and success for this networking approach.

8.3 Preparing for a Meeting

8.3.1 *Preparation starts long before the meeting itself*

When you do finally set up a meeting, it is important to prepare beforehand so that you can maximize the value that you get out of it. People's time is limited (and in their eyes, very valuable), and you will not be able to talk to them on an unlimited basis. In some cases, you will have no more than 15–20 minutes with someone (if they are willing to speak with you more, however, that's great). Before important meetings, we will typically spend at least ~30–60 minutes preparing (for more important meetings, this number can increase greatly).

The reason for this prep is to get the most out of the limited time with the person. You don't want to ask a question that you could quickly learn through Google, when that meeting time could be spent on another topic. You also want to make sure that what you ask is the best focus for the person you are meeting with. A side benefit to comprehensive preparation is that you will present yourself as collected and prepared. This might impress the person you are meeting, and make them more likely to want to work with you in the future.

To prepare, we will create a Google doc, where we will write down top objectives and questions. This document will also include some research on the person we are meeting. Objectives and questions will be ordered based on priority, in order to know what to discuss first. You can even practice introducing yourself in a succinct manner, so that you do not use a lot of time. This introduction can vary as well, based on who you are meeting and what experiences will be most relevant for the meeting you are having.

Example: Preparing for a Meeting

Every meeting is different, and how you prepare will vary from time to time. However, some of the core areas for preparation remain the same. The following are some general guidelines to apply to all meeting preparations.

It can be beneficial to save all notes in a Word or Google doc for reference. These notes will typically fall into three categories.

1. A tentative agenda

This is a quick, bullet point list of what you hope to accomplish during the meeting. For a 30-minute meeting, this usually contains 4–6

(*Continued*)

bullet points (plus some sub-sections if needed). This can help you plan how much time to spend on various topics, and ensure you cover all topics that you want to review.

Sometimes, something unexpected might come up, and the meeting will diverge from the planned agenda. This can be a positive thing, as long as the topic of discussion is beneficial. Don't be afraid to go "off-script" if this does come up, and the topic is of more interest than what you planned for. However, if it is not better, you can steer back to your original agenda.

2. The "Ask"

This section contains what you hope to get out of the meeting. There is no single type of "Ask" for all meetings — it might entail getting the answers to some questions you might have, or suggestions for future actions. It could also be the name of a contact or someone that would be beneficial to reach out to. A typical "Ask" is a list of ~3–5 bullet points. Make sure that what you are asking for is reasonable given the scope of your meeting, and who you are meeting with.

3. Pertinent information for this meeting

This is the least structured section, and contains any information that might be useful during the meeting. Some things you might include in this section:

- A personal introduction — this will often be tailored based on who you are meeting, emphasizing certain points of your background.
- Some background research on the person you are meeting, including anything that is particularly noteworthy.
- Questions you might want to ask. Even if you know what you want to ask/learn, it is good to write them out beforehand, in order to be efficient with your time.

(*Continued*)

(*Continued*)

> If possible, right before the meeting begins, it can be helpful to spend a few minutes reviewing these notes. That way, all content is fresh in your mind during the meeting itself. You can also print these notes if possible, though it is often not appropriate to be reading directly from a sheet of paper (it's great for phone or skype meetings though, if you can make glancing at them seem natural). However, preparation like this can ensure that you maximize the value of meetings when you have them.

8.3.2 *Always have an "Ask" — but make sure it's appropriate for the meeting*

You always want to have an objective for a meeting that you participate in. Otherwise, the meeting runs the risk of being unfocused and a potential waste of time. This can also be annoying to the person you are meeting with, decreasing the chance of future meetings.

What you can ask for depends greatly on the person you are contacting, and how extensive of a relationship you have with that person. If the person has a very busy work or travel schedule, don't ask for something that will take up a large amount of time. Further, if you are meeting someone for the first time, don't ask for too much (this should be saved for those with which you have a longstanding relationship).

There are some things you should **never** ask for when meeting someone for the first time. One common mistake new entrepreneurs make is asking for too much on the first meeting. For example, mentoring someone entails a large time commitment, and is usually driven by a personal connection between mentor and mentee. Most people won't commit a huge chunk of time to a person they have just met. Further, it's a bad idea to ask for funding during the first meeting with a potential investor (this usually occurs during a more formal funding pitch). The following table gives some

What to NOT ask for	Appropriate Alternative "Ask"	Rationale
Be your mentor	Advice on future actions	Effective mentorship entails a long-term and time-consuming commitment. Further, most mentorship is not created through structured set of actions, and people often do not respond positively to this request. It is better to develop a mentoring relationship slowly over time than to attempt to create it artificially. Asking for advice (as you would a mentor) is one approach to building this relationship.
Venture funding for your startup	Recommendations for fundraising strategies	Venture Capitalists spend a lot of time on analysis and due diligence before deciding to offer funding. You cannot complete this during the first meeting, and asking this will convey that your company is amateurish and unfamiliar with financing (which won't help your funding chances). Further, by asking for advice on fundraising, you are signaling that your startup will be looking for funding soon. If they are interested and a good fit, they will continue this topic of conversation.
An introduction to someone	Suggestions for who to reach out to for advice on a specified topic	When someone makes an introduction, they are tacitly endorsing you. If you end up screwing them over, it damages their reputation. Many people are aware of this,

(*Continued*)

(Continued)

What to NOT ask for	Appropriate Alternative "Ask"	Rationale
		and might be wary to do this for someone they just met. If you instead ask them for people to reach out to, they can then offer to make an introduction if they see fit.
Free products or services	Advice on how to obtain something in a cost-effective manner	While there are some resources available to startups for free, this should be seen as a rare exception and not the norm. Asking for something that normally costs money might put the person you are asking in an awkward position, making them less likely to work with you in the future. The best resources within a professional network are the ones that you can engage repeatedly, and this approach decreases the chance of this occurring.

examples of things to never ask for during the first meeting, and a better alternative to ask for to pursue that goal.

Asking for too much isn't the only mistake one can make. Some entrepreneurs will ask for things that might be inappropriate. For example, if you are meeting someone that works for a potential competitor, it might put them in a weird spot to ask for something that will directly impact the business they work for (and they will likely have to say no to). This is another reason why it's important to do research before a meeting begins.

During the meeting itself, it is sometimes beneficial to briefly introduce an agenda at the start of the meeting. Even if time is scarce, 30–60 seconds can be enough to do so. Presenting your agenda might give you a better chance of getting through all action items in a set amount of time, and not run over. The people you meet with will be busy — sometimes they will have to leave at the end of the scheduled time, whether you cover everything or not. Further, it will help ensure that you do not focus the entire time on a single topic, and leave time for everything planned.

8.3.3 *Post-meeting actions*

As a kid, your mother probably told you to write a thank you note when someone did something nice for you (you might or might not have listened to this advice). However, this can be a good idea after you meet with someone. This person has volunteered their time to help you with something, and it's good to show your appreciation. Further, if you met someone that you want to maintain a long-term professional relationship with, this appreciation will make it more likely that this will occur. So, when it comes to thank you notes, your mother was right — you should call her to tell her that (she will appreciate this).

8.4 Conclusion

A robust professional network is an important source of support for entrepreneurs. It can provide expertise, access to sales channels and partnerships, and mentorship that they otherwise couldn't obtain. While there are diverse ways to develop a professional network (as discussed in this chapter), it is important that you are constantly maintaining and adding to this network.

Some people are shy about meeting new contacts, and find networking actions daunting. The best advice we can give to get over this hurdle is to go out and undertake some real-world networking actions. This approach is very similar to the experiential learning emphasized during 3DS programs, and is one of the most effective ways to become more comfortable with networking actions. It may seem challenging at first, but it gets a lot easier the more you do this. The importance of developing a professional network should outweigh any apprehension that entrepreneurs have.

If you are still shy or worried about this approach, you can initially try this with a connection that will have a lower value to you. That way, if you mess up or don't do well, you can learn from the experience, and do better with higher value contacts in the future. No one learns networking skills overnight, and it is important to be continually refining and improving these skills for your career.

Further, networking in an imperfect art, and no one achieves 100% success rate. You will meet people that you initially think will be a great help to your professional efforts that ultimately turn out to not be very helpful. Sometimes, you will contact people and never hear back from them (especially when cold calling). However, *when* (not *if*) this occurs, you cannot become dejected and give up growing your professional network. It must be a continual, consistent process to expand possible connections to help build your startup.

Finally, your professional network is not a one-way street, and you cannot only receive help from network contacts. In this chapter, we primarily discussed how to grow and maintain contacts that will help you during your entrepreneurial endeavors. However, you should also consider how you can contribute to others that might reach out to you for similar help. Entrepreneurs should strive to make their connections mutually beneficial. This will help ensure your contacts will remain active and responsive, and can provide additional help in the future.

Part 4

Balancing Entrepreneurship with Other Aspects of Life

Chapter 9

Maximizing Entrepreneurial Learning as a Student

9.1 Introduction

Post-secondary education is one of the few times in your adult life when one's main focus is learning and personal development. For young people aspiring to become entrepreneurs, it can be a formative time that teaches the skills necessary for future business creation actions. This development will manifest from many different sources — while you will likely focus on a certain major or degree program, this is not the only educational pursuit you will need to undertake during this time to become a successful adult or entrepreneur. No major or degree plan contains all information needed for a comprehensive successful career. This is especially true of multidisciplinary fields like entrepreneurship. As an entrepreneur (or entrepreneurially minded employee), you will have to train yourself to wear many "hats" and successfully complete tasks in a variety of fields.

Post-secondary institutions have many resources to help young entrepreneurs grow both inside and outside the classroom. In addition to coursework, there are many extracurricular clubs and programs for further learning. Additionally, human capital, comprising both professors and your fellow classmates, can be a great source of help and future business partnerships. Beyond the school or college itself, there are also many special programs like jobs and internships specifically aimed at helping students learn and grow. It is important to pursue all of these avenues as a student to gain a comprehensive, well-rounded education that will launch a successful early career.

Many people incorrectly assume that all learning and development comes from the classroom. Subsequently, many students do not pursue as many great extracurricular and off-campus opportunities as they could or should. One major frustration we have is that most post-secondary institutions do not adequately emphasize or prioritize extra-curricular student development, further adding to this problem. However, this represents only a portion of personal development opportunities, and students that make the most of their time as a student take a comprehensive, multifaceted approach, looking for multiple sources of learning. This is why it is important to get outside your dorm room (and classroom), and take advantage of as many of these resources as you can during your relatively short time as a student.

To succeed in any career field, including those outside of entrepreneurship, you will have to continually teach yourself new skills. This learning style is different from classroom learning, and is largely self-driven. Even if you maintain the same job position/function, your responsibilities will change over time, and you will have to adapt to these changes. Further, jobs are changing more quickly than they did in the past. This is why 3 Day Startup (3DS) places a huge emphasis on "learning by doing" and practicing the skills we introduce to participants. While we do use short educational modules to introduce content, most learning occurs from participants trying out skills and learning from direct experiences. Studying at a post-secondary institution is a great time to grow from informal learning environments, and this chapter will introduce how to take advantage of extracurricular activities, interacting with fellow classmates, and pursuing off-campus opportunities.

In this chapter, we introduce what you can do as a student to develop your entrepreneurial skills, as well as a fledgling venture you might have. We look at what can be done both inside and outside of the classroom for this development. While this chapter is aimed at current or soon-to-be students, this advice does not solely apply to this audience. Many of the topics and actions introduced can be applied to non-academic settings as well. They might need some tweaking to be relevant, but by no means should you automatically skip this chapter if you are not currently a student.

Should You Drop Out of School to Work on Your Startup?

There are many that believe that entrepreneurs don't need a formal education to be successful. In extreme cases, this can mean dropping out or forgoing post-secondary education in the first place. Some are even actively encouraging people to drop out and focus on entrepreneurship — Peter Theil created the Theil Fellowship, which offers $100,000 to student-age entrepreneurs to pursue their venture full time.[1,2] While there are merits to both sides of this topic, at 3DS we get asked about this topic frequently, and feel the need to address it.

There are some potential advantages to pursuing entrepreneurship over education. Learning by doing is a highly effective method of learning, and is especially true for entrepreneurship. Entrepreneurs are constantly learning new things (partially out of necessity) as they develop their new business. Schoolwork also takes time away from one's business, and many want to focus on their venture full time. Finally, there is significant concern about student debt, and many do not want to take on large loans if it is not critical to successful entrepreneurship. This student debt can be a hindrance to entrepreneurship, as it can pressure recent graduates to pursue higher-paying, non-entrepreneurial job tracks out of financial necessity.

However, this line of thinking overlooks the multiple downsides of forgoing post-secondary education. While you will not learn

---

(Continued)

(*Continued*)

everything necessary, you can develop many entrepreneurial skills as a student. This can be optimized by steering your studies in ways that focus on entrepreneurship (we elaborate on this more extensively later in the chapter). There are also many great opportunities exclusively for students, including extracurricular clubs and activities as well as internships.

Finally, it is important to note the highly volatile nature of startups, and that many businesses fail, even when the founder does everything correctly. Depending on who conducts the study, startup failure rates range between 70–90%.[3] People like to mention success stories of dropout-founders like Bill Gates and Steve Jobs. However, they fail to notice the even greater number of business failures that occurred at the same time.[4] Do you remember Friendster? (Don't Google it — that's cheating) Orkut? Yahoo Buzz? Almost everyone knows about Facebook, but can't name many of the dozens of failed social networks that came before it. Survivorship bias is a term to describe this phenomenon, when unsuccessful cases are not considered due to lack of visibility.

When we deliver 3DS programs, some of our participants discover that they do not want to become founders of a business (though many more realize they do, or increase their extant interest in the field). Things like long work hours, below market salaries, limited benefits, and minimal job security all weigh on people, and they realize the life of a founder is not for them. This is a completely fine choice, and there are many productive, meaningful career paths outside of entrepreneurship. However, if you end up in this category, having a degree will help immensely with whatever career path you end up on.

Overall, we do not advocate dropping out to focus fully on a business. While post-secondary institutions need to improve how they deliver entrepreneurship education, there is still value in these institutions for aspiring entrepreneurs. Instead, we recommend that you spend your time as a student making the most of your entrepreneurial development. This chapter contains some strategies and tips to help with this endeavor.

(*Continued*)

(*Continued*)

One exception to this recommendation is those considering additional studies. Often, we will meet people considering additional entrepreneurship education (like an MBA), but who are unsure about how this might be beneficial. In this case, it is perfectly fine to put off this new education to spend additional time figuring out if this will be a benefit to future career actions.

9.2 Why Post-Secondary Institutions are a Great Place to Develop Entrepreneurially

9.2.1 *Your coursework can teach you many (but not all) skills that you will need as an entrepreneur*

A large portion of your time as a student will be spent taking coursework within a certain major. This major can focus on an entrepreneurship-related field, and help teach you some of the skills needed for successful business creation. To maximize value of your major, it is important to pick a degree program that you believe will be pertinent to entrepreneurship. This doesn't have to be business-related — as we noted before, entrepreneurship is a multidisciplinary field, and there are many educational paths to approach. When considering a major to help entrepreneurial aspirations, consider your desired career path, the field you want to go into, and how the skills acquired in that major will assist future entrepreneurial actions.

Beyond your major, you will also have time for electives and other courses of your choosing. This is further opportunity to acquire skills critical for being a successful entrepreneur. In particular, it can be a valuable chance to explore topics in a field different from your major, building your multidisciplinary skillset. In this situation, many people choose classes that seem interesting, or things that are "an easy A." While this can leave more time for other courses, it also often represents a missed opportunity for additional learning.

Example: Stanford University Symbolic Systems Major

Symbolic Systems is a major at Stanford University that focuses on minds (both biological and artificial), and how these minds use symbols to communicate and represent information. It also looks into how humans interact with computers, and how to make these interactions as seamless as possible. With software and human-computer interactions becoming ubiquitous in all fields, the material taught in this major has widespread applications in design, business, research, and public service.

One unique and powerful aspect of this major and its alumni is the multidisciplinary approach the degree program takes. Instead of approaching content from a single field (like Computer Science), students in this degree program take courses in Computer Science, Philosophy, Linguistics, and Psychology. This is incredibly useful when creating products or services for end users. For example, when creating human-computer interfaces, it is beneficial to know not only the programming skills required to create the interface, but also human psychology to ensure that it is intuitive for its end-users.

As a result of its multidisciplinary approach, it is not surprising that many Symbolic Systems majors go on to be successful entrepreneurs. Mark Zuckerberg even said that Symbolic Systems majors "were among the most talented people in the world." The following table lists some (but by far not all) of the most notable personnel with degrees in Symbolic Systems.

Alumni	Notable for
Reid Hoffman	Cofounder and Chairman of LinkedIn
Marissa Mayor	CEO of Yahoo
Mike Krieger (BS and MS)	Founder of Instagram
Scott Forstall	Apple executive, Advisor to Snapchat
Chris Cox	Chief Product Officer, Facebook
Srini Srinivasan	5th employee at Yahoo, Stanford Board of Trustees

9.2.2 *Opportunities to steer coursework to maximize entrepreneurial development*

The term "Double Dipping" often refers to receiving credit or compensation twice for a single action or piece of work. It is sometimes perceived as unethical or illegal (especially in cases where income or payment is involved), and is often frowned upon. However, there are positive (and completely ethical) applications for this concept, including those involving the use of coursework to promote your entrepreneurial development.

Many classes have assignments or final projects where students can pursue a topic of their choosing. These can be used to further explore a topic of interest, or even work on a project that can develop your startup. This allows you to develop business skills or your business while receiving course credit. It also allows you to get help and feedback from professors running the class, and tap into their expertise. Subsequently, double dipping for developing your business can be a significant asset.

9.2.3 *Extracurricular activities provide opportunities for additional learning*

Many students do not consider extracurricular activities as part of their education. They might believe that it is not an "official" part of school, since it does not lead to course credit or a diploma, and is therefore a lesser priority. However, extracurricular activities can be as impactful as coursework for entrepreneurial development and growth. At 3DS programs, we will often have students tell us things like: "I learned more in 3DS than I did in an entire semester of classes", or "3DS was the most educational experience I had in school." Additionally, many of our alumni tell us that 3DS inspired them to pursue other entrepreneurship-related coursework and extracurricular activities. Subsequently, extracurricular activities, including those which are not affiliated with your college or university — can serve as an important part of your education.

Schools will have many official and unofficial clubs focused on entrepreneurship. These will give you opportunities to learn more about business creation. It is also a chance to meet other entrepreneurially minded people. Examples of different types of extracurricular activities include the following:

- Non-credit-earning classes and educational workshops (like 3DS).
- Entrepreneurship-themed conferences (like Harvard's SPARK Entrepreneurship Conference).[5]
- Guest speakers and seminars that frequently visit campuses.
- Student clubs (like local chapters of Collegiate Entrepreneurs' Organization (CEO)).[6]
- Business plan competitions like University of Nebraska's New Venture Competition.[7]

One potential advantage of these extracurriculars is that many will be free or highly subsidized, and cost students little to nothing other than time. While there is free programming outside of colleges and universities, it is much harder to come across. Further, many schools have a diverse range of events and activities to choose from. This allows you to pursue multidisciplinary options, and provides the opportunity to select the ones that best match your intended focus of development.

For all these extracurricular opportunities, it is up to you to identify what you will attend. You should actively be searching for new opportunities in addition to your coursework. Additionally, you should focus on opportunities that best fit your interests and desired career path. For example, Yale University has many different entrepreneurship-related clubs and organizations.[8] If you were interested in designing new products that would lead to viable ventures, you might consider the Design + Innovation Club. Alternatively, if you are interested in Social Entrepreneurship, Yale Undergraduate Net Impact, which focuses on bridging business and social sectors, might be a better fit. You will be the person most knowledgeable about your personal and career interests, and therefore, the best judge of what clubs and organizations will be the best fit.

9.2.4 *Off-campus opportunities exclusively for students*

Up until now, we have discussed personal development opportunities that happen on campuses, or are affiliated with the institutions that students attend. However, this is not the full extent of extracurricular entrepreneurial opportunities available for students. It is also important to consider off-campus opportunities as a source for personal growth outside the classroom.

Part-time jobs and internships are a great way to learn professional skills. A good internship experience will have you working on an actual business project, and learning experientially within a business or organization. You will also get to see how the organization operates, and how multiple employees or teams work together towards a single goal. Another benefit of jobs and internships is that they are usually designed with a natural ending date, making it a great way to experientially investigate a skill, type of job, or career path that you might be interested in. If you learn that it is not a good fit, you can move on to other pursuits after its natural end.

Example: Austin Technology Incubator's Summer Entrepreneurship Acceleration and Launch (SEAL) Program

Austin Technology Incubator (ATI) is a startup incubator located in Austin Texas. Over the last 25 years, they have helped local startups raise over $600 million in investment funding. They are a robust and important part of the Austin startup ecosystem, and many successful ventures attribute their success in part due to their guidance. They are also highly selective, and accept only 8–10% of all companies that apply.[9]

In addition to their main accelerator programs, ATI has a special program exclusively for students called the Summer Entrepreneur Acceleration and Launch (SEAL). This nine-week course takes place over the summer, and helps students rapidly get to a "go/no

---

(*Continued*)

(Continued)

go" decision for their venture. ATI provides mentorship and other program resources for the students in this course.[10]

This student program is generally easier to get into than the regular incubator program. And while the SEAL program doesn't go in as much depth as the traditional accelerator, students have access to the same mentors and incubator resources.

There are many other incubator and accelerator programs (like Stanford's StartX[11] and MIT's delta v[12]) that have similar programs that are exclusively for students. Aspiring student entrepreneurs should look out for these opportunities both on and off campus as an opportunity to further their entrepreneurial development.

9.2.5 *The importance of being proactive when pursuing extracurricular opportunities*

As described above, there are many opportunities both inside and outside the classroom to help your entrepreneurial development as a student. Beyond the classes required for your academic major and graduation, you will have the opportunity to choose additional classes to take as a student. Further, you will have significant time outside of class that you can devote to informal learning opportunities. The key to taking advantage of many of these opportunities is to be proactive, and take initiative for those that you are interested in. It will be up to you to identify the most productive optional class and extracurricular activities. Further, you will know best what you need to grow into a successful entrepreneur. Therefore, you should be in the driver's seat as much as possible when seeking opportunities as a student.

Further reason to be proactive is that there are few reasons to not do so. In many cases the worst that can happen is that you are told "no", or that an opportunity is not available. While rejection can be demoralizing, it is a recurring part of entrepreneurship and you should not be discouraged by it. A very prominent startup mentor once told me, "If you don't hear no at least once in a while, you are not trying hard enough as an entrepreneur." Subsequently, fear of rejection should not deter you from trying for beneficial opportunities.

What to Do if an Opportunity is Full

Sometimes, you will find an amazing opportunity — i.e. a really interesting class, a workshop introducing a technique you want to learn, or a cool conference in town — only to discover that it is completely full. Maybe the program is highly competitive (the best ones usually are), or you found out about it late. This doesn't mean you should give up on taking part in this opportunity — you can still ask if there is any way you are able to take part. The following are some tips you can use when asking about a full or otherwise unavailable opportunity:

1. Act REALLY enthusiastic when you ask.

People like to work with those that are passionate about the subject matter they are delivering. Acting really enthusiastic will make them more likely to want to work with you, and try to find an exception that might be able to accommodate you. Therefore, when reaching out about a potential opportunity, you want to act as enthusiastic as possible about said opportunity.

2. Look for any possible way (even unconventional ones) to participate.

For a really valuable opportunity, you should be interested in any way to gain exposure, even if it is not the originally envisioned embodiment. Be open to alternate ideas. For example, if you really want to learn from an elective class, ask if you can audit it and not receive credit.

3. Ask if you can get on the waitlist.

Sometimes, others will drop out or never show up, leading to an unexpected opening. If you ask to be put on a waitlist, you might be the first person they call if a spot opens up.

(Continued)

(Continued)

4. When reaching out, prepare beforehand, so that you are mindful of others' time.

When reaching out to someone, don't just rattle off all questions that come to mind. Do some initial preparation, so that you don't ask a question that can be solved by internet research.

5. Be persistent, yet polite

Keep in mind that you are asking for something outside the norm. As a result. If an initial email for attempt at contact doesn't get a response, try contacting them again. Don't be rude or batter them with endless questions — that will just annoy them and make them less likely to accommodate you.

6. If unsuccessful, don't hesitate to try again

These tips will help, but they won't work every time. If you can't get in this time around, there might a second date or occurrence for the opportunity. Offer to come back at a later date. Finally, remember when we told you "if you don't hear no at least once in a while, you're not trying hard enough"? This sentiment applies to this situation as well.

9.3 Human Capital within a Post-Secondary Education Ecosystem

One frequently-overlooked benefit of being a student is the opportunity to meet and interact with other like-minded individuals. Colleges and universities have a high concentration of human capital that is not usually replicated in other settings. It is possible to meet others outside of academic settings, though this can be much more challenging and time-consuming than as a student. It can be harder to track down the exact people you're looking for, and doing so consumes much of your time. Further, students are generally more open-minded to meeting new people. As a result, one productive use of your time as a student entails meeting your fellow students and adding like-minded ones to your professional network.

9.3.1 *Your fellow classmates are an amazing resource*

As a student, you will be in contact with many other young ambitious people, and gain exposure to diverse perspectives you wouldn't encounter otherwise. You will also meet others interested in entrepreneurship, who will likely be your colleagues in the future. The ones with complementary interests and skillsets might also become your future cofounders and business partners.

At 3DS, we often hear that one of the most valuable parts of the program is connecting with 40 other entrepreneurially minded individuals. There are few other opportunities where they get to interact with so many entrepreneurial-minded individuals in such a short time period. These meetings are not only recreational though — many times, participants that meet at 3DS go on to become cofounders, business partners, and collaborators years after program completion. The friendships you make at school can help drive your journey in business as well, and should not be overlooked as a benefit of post-secondary education.

9.3.2 *Your professors can be helpful as well*

Professors are another asset that many students don't fully take advantage of during their studies. If you are taking their class, they likely have expertise in a field that is of interest to you. Professors are also often interested in interacting with students, and will be open to discussing topics of interest outside of class. This makes professors a potentially valuable resource, and one you should talk to about questions beyond homework and exams.

Many professors have office hours where students can "drop in" and ask questions. This is a great way to learn about topics both inside and outside of the class. If professors don't have a time when you can drop in, you can email them to set a time to meet up. The following is a template one can use to reach out to professors for similar issues.

Email Body	Commentary (Related to underlined text)
Dear Professor NAME,	
<u>My name is NAME, and I am a student in your CLASS.</u>	This introduction might not be necessary for smaller classes or times when a professor already knows who you are. But an introduction helps give some context when reaching out to them.
<u>I have a strong interest in TOPIC, and am seriously considering a career which focuses on JOB after graduation.</u> While I very much enjoy your CLASS, I am hoping to further explore how TOPIC ties into jobs in industry/entrepreneurship.	Tying their class to your post-graduation career here attempts to pique their interest and increase the chance of a positive response.
<u>Is there a time I can ask you a couple of questions about TOPIC?</u> I am happy to come to your office during scheduled office hours, or another time that is convenient for you.	Be flexible, and give your professor options for times to meet.
Thank you, NAME	

When you do finally schedule a time with a professor, you should prepare before this meeting takes place. Brainstorm questions and the general objectives for this meeting. The reasons for this are twofold. First, professors have limited time, and you will not be able to ask unlimited questions. Also, when you prepare before a meeting, your demeanor in that meeting is more likely to appear collected and articulate. You are more likely to impress your professors when you meet with them, and they are more likely to want to work with you further.

9.3.3 *Building your personal network as a student*

Entrepreneurs will constantly be building and expanding their professional network (this is actually true for ALL career fields, but in this book, we are focused primarily on entrepreneurship). These connections can turn into future mentors, business partners, and sources of support that will be critical to future entrepreneurial success.

As a student, one effective way to build your professional network is to be active in your classes and extracurricular activities. This will get you interacting with other students and professors, and building relationships that will help you beyond graduation. However, these actions by themselves are not enough, and you should also be pursuing new connections with those outside of class and off campus. This can be a bit trickier, as you won't just run into these people during your daily routine, and you must initiate these meetings. However, there is no secret technique or skill for successful networking, and being a student can sometimes help facilitate these meetings.

Building a professional network is a broad enough topic that it could be its own book chapter (in fact, Chapter 8 "Building a professional network" is dedicated to this topic). However, you should know that students can make great progress starting their professional network for their future career. Even though this isn't as concrete as other entrepreneurial activities, it is still important and should be considered during one's career as a student.

9.4 How to Skip a Class: A Tutorial

So you've finally set up a great opportunity: maybe it's a free pass to a cool entrepreneurship conference, or a one-on-one meeting with an ideal potential mentor. The one downside is that the only time this can take place requires you to miss a class. You've tried rescheduling, but for whatever reason, there is no way to avoid a conflict and miss something. Fortunately, we are going to review how to navigate this situation as unobtrusively as possible.

9.4.1 *Make it count — you only get to do this so many times*

Opportunity cost is the loss of other potential gains that you forgo when pursuing something. For example, if you go to a pizza restaurant for dinner, you are forgoing the opportunity to eat at a Mexican restaurant, barbecue joint, or to cook a meal at home. If you are really in the mood for pizza, the benefits of doing this outweigh the cost of the other eating options, and this is a net benefit. However, if you would get more benefit from eating another type of food, it might be better to consider something else.

You should consider the opportunity cost any time you might miss a class for another opportunity. Is this opportunity more important than what you will be missing? Is there a way to minimize what is lost?

While this tutorial can help mitigate the opportunity cost of missing a class, it cannot be done infinitely. The first or second time you skip class, your professor might understand. However, if it continues beyond then, they might begin to believe that you don't prioritize their course. Consequently, really consider the opportunity, and if it is worth skipping a class.

Right now, you might be thinking "this is great, I can use this for a party/concert/long weekend." And the truth is, noone is going to stop you — after all, you're an adult. But you shouldn't do this, because it can hinder your personal development as you grow into an entrepreneur. Previously, we have mentioned time as a constrained resource, and you should always do what will help your nascent entrepreneurial career the most. That being said, we recognize the importance of self-care and mental well-being. Continue to pursue those concerts/parties but not at the expense of coursework or other personal development opportunities.

9.4.2 *Plan ahead: This goes a lot better if done before the event than afterwards*

If you are going to miss a class, it is important to have a plan for how to make up anything you are missing. This does not have to be overly complex or intricate — it can be as simple as "Get notes from a friend, ask the TA if you have any further questions". But having a plan in place gives you a roadmap for proceeding as efficiently as possible.

Further, if you contact a professor beforehand, it implicitly sends the message that you prioritize the class and are thinking about it at an early stage. If there is anything important your professor wants you to do before skipping a class, advance notification allows for more flexibility for makeup options. Sometimes there is no other option but to complete things late (like homework assignments and tests), and this is the only way to make up work. Even if you ultimately make up something after missing the class, the earlier you know, the easier it will be to plan around it. In general, it is good to leave at least a week's notice before the date in question. Sometimes, giving less notice might be unavoidable. In these situations, notification sooner rather than later is better.

9.4.2.1 *Reaching out to a professor*

Various forms of the following email can be used when reaching out in regards to a missed class or similar function:

Email Body	Commentary (Related to Underlined Text)
Dear Professor NAME,	
Next week, I have an exciting opportunity to [quick intro to opportunity]. Unfortunately, it takes place at TIME, and I will have to miss the class.	When describing the opportunity, try to make it sound like you are interested in the class.
While I value and prioritize class, I am unable to reschedule this meeting, and it seems like a rare opportunity that I shouldn't miss.	This pre-empts a possible response from your professor to just reschedule the other meeting.

(*Continued*)

(*Continued*)

Email Body	Commentary (Related to Underlined Text)
I would still like to make up the content that I will be missing on my own time. <u>I have asked a friend to share their class notes with me from the lecture I am missing</u>. In addition to this, I will follow up with the course TA if I have any remaining questions after reviewing this material.	This shows you planning ahead, and signals that you are being proactive and not skipping class on a whim.
Finally, I will not be able to turn in my homework due to not being in class that day. <u>Would it possible to turn it into a TA or slip it under your door before the DUE DATE?</u> Please let me know what course of action would be least obtrusive.	This paragraph might not apply if you are not missing a time to turn in assignments. However, always offer to turn in things **before** the due date rather than **after**. That way, it doesn't look like you are asking for an extension or special treatment.
Appreciatively, NAME	

While it is good to have a plan, you professor might offer additional suggestions about how to make up anything you will be missing. Additionally, if your professor asks you to meet with them or a TA in the course, you should do so. They are accommodating a special request, and you should do whatever they believe is best. Further, they might be going out of their way to help you. If they ask you to show up at their office hours, make time when it is convenient for them. Come prepared to talk about the opportunity and your plan to make up the coursework you will miss. You do not want to waste their time.

Example: How Student Athletes Miss Class for Sporting Events

Student athletics at the collegiate level can be extremely time-consuming. When in season (and frequently when not in season) they are practicing and training for multiple hours every day. Additionally, they are frequently traveling to go to games and competitions at other schools. Not surprisingly, this can lead to many conflicts and missing classes at various times.

Due to NCAA (National Collegiate Athletic Association — the organization that oversees college sports in the US) regulations, student-athletes must have minimal disruptions to their academic schedules. As a result, many athletic programs have a lot of steps in place to help minimize the scheduling conflicts from this travel. At the start of their collegiate careers, athletes are given training for best practices to manage these conflicts. Many schools have created a template letter which athletes can pass on to their professors when conflicts arise. This letter explains why the travel is an important endeavor for the institution, and how the student plans to make up missed work.

Many institutions also hire special academic advisors to help athletes coordinate turning in assignments and rescheduling quizzes and tests. Finally, many schools will also hire tutors to help students make up missed classes.

This example can serve as a case study for how to approach missing a class. You might not have access to these exact resources, but similar ones might be available to you. Try and identify support systems within your school that can be helpful when you miss a class for another important opportunity.

9.5 Conclusion

Post-secondary education is a time of rapid personal development, and will provide many opportunities for aspiring entrepreneurs to develop capabilities important to their future career. These opportunities will come from multiple places, including classroom learning; interactions with fellow classmates and professors; extracurricular activities on campus; and special off-campus opportunities exclusively for students. Students should be open to opportunities for entrepreneurial development in all embodiments. Further, the high concentration of human capital found at post-secondary institutions allows you to meet people that can become part of your professional network, and should not be overlooked during your studies.

One downside to this high concentration of opportunities is that you will not have the time to pursue everything. It is important to consider time as a valuable, limited asset. Further, you must consider the opportunity cost of all opportunities, and what you might otherwise be missing. For these considerations, you will know best about the most productive uses of your time, and what will be most beneficial to your development as an entrepreneur.

To take full advantage of these opportunities, you will have to be proactive and take initiative on your own. Many of the best programs are optional, and take place outside of classes required for your major. It will be up to you to identify and pursue these opportunities.

References

1. McAlone, N. (2015, June 6). Billionaire Peter Thiel is giving these 20 kids $100,000 to drop out of college and start companies. *INSIDER.* Retrieved from https://www.businessinsider.com/meet-the-2015-thiel-fellows-2015-6
2. *Thiel Fellowship.* (n.d.). Retrieved from Wikipedia: https://en.wikipedia.org/wiki/Thiel_Fellowship#cite_note-2015-release-1.
3. https://hbr.org/2021/05/why-start-ups-fail.
4. Zimmer, R. J. (2013, March 1). The Myth of the Successful College Dropout: Why It Could Make Millions of Young Americans Poorer. *The Atlantic.* Retrieved from https://www.theatlantic.com/business/archive/2013/03/the-myth-of-the-successful-college-dropout-why-it-could-make-millions-of-young-americans-poorer/273628/.
5. https://www.hbs.edu/mba/student-life/activities-government-and-clubs/Pages/other-activities.aspx.
6. Collegiate Entrepreneurs Organization. (n.d.). Retrieved from http://c-e-o.site-ym.com/?

7. https://business.unl.edu/academic-programs/center-for-entrepre-neurship/student-programs-and-competition/.

8. http://yei.yale.edu/student-entrepreneurship-clubs-and-organizations.

9. Austin Technology Incubator. (n.d.). Retrieved from Austin Technology Incubator — The University of Texas at Austin: https://ati.utexas.edu/.

10. Austin Technology Incubator. (n.d.). *SEAL Accelerator*. Retrieved from Austin Technology Incubator — The University of Texas at Austin: https://ati.utexas.edu/seal/.

11. StartX. (n.d.). Retrieved from StartX: https://startx.com/

12. Massachusetts Institute of Technology. (n.d.). *MIT delta v Educational Accelarator*. Retrieved from The Martin Trust Center for MIT Entrepreneurship: https://entrepreneurship.mit.edu/accelerator/program/.

Chapter 10

Growing your Startup While Keeping your Day Job

10.1 Introduction: You're Not Ready to Work on Your Startup Full Time

For many entrepreneurs, dedicating all of your working hours to a startup is the ultimate goal (short of an IPO or buyout, where you're doing the same thing while also receiving lots of money). However, this status does not happen instantaneously, and you will have to grow your business over time.

In the early stages of most startups, founders will not take any salary so that money is not taken out of the business. Many startups initially don't have revenue, and even those that do are often not profitable (yet). Even when a startup is cash flow positive (i.e. more money is coming into the company than going out of it), it is not enough to pay a full-time salary. Subsequently, founders and early employees of a startup must look elsewhere for personal funds during this initial growth period.

Even when a startup can support salaries for one or more full-time employees, there can be compelling reasons for not doing so. It is often advantageous to re-invest business profits into growing the business further. Remember, startups can grow fast, and reinvesting profits can help fuel this rapid growth. Forgoing salary can also help with fundraising strategies. Startups that aren't paying salaries can put off fundraising for longer, leaving more time to develop the business. Further, it can help get more favorable investment terms and company valuations (by allowing companies to wait for better offers). As a result, many founders forgo salary and hiring employees even when it is not necessary to do so.

It's a romantic notion to sacrifice payment to help fund a startup you are passionate about. However, romantic notions don't pay for rent or groceries. While some founders live off their savings for a time, most will probably need another source of income as they grow their business. Many people elect to work elsewhere full or part-time in the early days of their startup, and must balance multiple responsibilities when growing their fledgling business.

Further, having another job during the early stages of startup development can help mitigate the volatility of fledgling startups. Some startups are bound to fail, even when founders do everything correctly. Other times, founders might not be sure if a business concept can become a profitable business, and is worth pursuing. Keeping a day job during these early, unpredictable stages allows founders to have something to fall back on in case their startup doesn't grow as hoped into a successful business.

Finally, leaving a full-time job to work on a startup is a major decision, and one that should not be made lightly. Even if a founder is confident to take the plunge fully into their startup, some planning should be done before doing so. Many founders like to build up their savings, and get personal and professional affairs in order before proceeding. Doing two things at once allows founders to prepare for this milestone to minimize the chaos of this transition as much as possible.

In this chapter, we discuss some important ideas and strategies for growing a startup while maintaining a "day job" or other source of income. We will introduce some common pitfalls, and tips for how to avoid conflicts between your day job and startup. We will also discuss time management, and making the most of your limited time. Finally, we will introduce outsourcing and other strategies to maximize the rate of progress during this phase.

10.2 Balancing Two Jobs at Once

10.2.1 *Don't blur the lines between your day job and your startup*

Many founders keep working at their day job during the initial period of starting a business, and it is very feasible to have two jobs at once. However, it is important to keep clear boundaries between the two efforts. When you are working at a job, someone else is paying you for your efforts. During the time you are being paid, your employer is allocating resources (including your time) to accomplish something of their choosing. It would be unethical to use that time or other employer resources for tasks that are not beneficial to the employer (like building your startup).

Further, many organizations have an official policy against using company resources for personal benefit, including building your startup. These resources include company equipment (i.e. computers, machinery), as well as time when the company is paying you to work on other tasks. Some companies even have employees sign legally binding statements agreeing to this policy. Penalties for violating these clauses can be harsh — you can lose your job, or the company can make a claim on ownership of your startup. Even if these don't occur, it can create a lot of bad feelings between you and your employer, and reduce the potency of your professional network. Even though it can seem tempting to use these resources as "free help," you should not do so for ethical and pragmatic reasons.

A further reason to not blur boundaries is that you will get less done. Research has confirmed that humans are less productive when multitasking than when focusing on a single task at a time.[1] It is much better to work on one task for a block of time, then switch over to a second one. With all these reasons, it is important that you have separate times for your current job and the startup you are trying to build.

As you are reading this advice, you might be thinking "But didn't you tell us double dipping was a good thing in Chapter 9?" The answer to that is yes — yes we did. However, there is an important difference between what we were advocating in that chapter, and what is being discussed here. As a student, you are not being paid to attend (usually you are the one doing the paying). It is therefore not unethical to direct your schoolwork to help bolster your other professional goals. This is not the case for a salaried position, and you are ethically and legally obligated to use it for the purpose your employer designates.

10.3 Managing Time Effectively

One theme continually repeated within this book is that time is a limited resource. While it is true of all founders, it is especially true of those with both a startup and a day job. In addition to growing a business, you are allocating ~40 (or even more) hours per week to a day job. You will have to find new and creative ways to set aside time to devote to building your startup.

If you work a full-time job, it's likely that most of your time during business hours (~9:00–5:00 on weekdays) will be dedicated to that position. However, there are still a lot of other blocks of time that you can dedicate to your startup. There are 168 hours in a week. A full-time job will take up ~40–60 hours, depending on the position. You will probably need to sleep 42–56 hours (~6–8 hours/night), and dedicate another 10–15 hours to continue being a healthy adult (giving up showers to save time is not worth it — don't learn this experientially, just take our word on it). This leaves 37–76 hours of time per week which you can dedicate to your startup. You're probably not a robot, and will not be able to allocate all of those hours to developing your startup. However, it still leaves plenty of opportunities to work and make progress.

Many entrepreneurs become skilled at finding non-traditional hours to work on tasks related to building their startup. For example, some like to wake up early, and have some time for productivity before their "day job" begins. Others like working in the evening after they put their kids to bed. Sometimes, founders will even use vacation time to dedicate a full block of time to their startup alone.

There is no single best time to work on your startup, as long as you are able to find time when you can be productive.

This process can seem confusing and challenging to some people. However, this non-traditional work cycle is also appealing to many that work for startups. They enjoy the freedom of having a non-rigid work schedule, and having the flexibility to pause for life or other opportunities.

Further, even if you don't have a set time or schedule to work on your startup, it is crucial that you dedicate consistent time to developing your startup. The ultimate goal is to create a sustainable startup that will continue to grow until profitability. Subsequently, you cannot envision a startup like a school assignment or one-time work project. Making consistent progress is much more important than short, intense spurts of work.

While having a flexible schedule can be enjoyable, as an entrepreneur, you have to supervise your own actions and hold yourself accountable. If you put off working on your startup, it is likely that no one will notice or call you out. This can be especially appealing, since one can argue to prioritize a paying job over their startup "side project." However, this will severely limit the development of your business venture, and possibly contribute to its failure.

Finally, you will probably have to give up or limit the amount of time dedicated to certain activities to make time for working on your startup. You might have to reduce the amount of times you socialize with friends from three times per week to once per week. Alternatively, you might not sleep in every day of the weekend. However, this does not mean you will have to give up these things completely — it just means you will have to limit some time allocated to certain activities other than your day job and startup development.

As an example, an entrepreneur the authors mentored in Lincoln liked to spend a long time at the gym. A typical workout included 20 minutes of stretching/warmup, 40 minutes of cardio, 30 minutes in the steam room, and some socialization for a total of ~2 hours per session. However, once he started developing his business, this became a consistent time strain that started eating into work time for his business. He didn't want to give up going to the gym completely. Instead, he started doing much more accelerated workouts — a quick 5-minute warmup, 40 minutes of cardio, a quick shower, then back to work ~1 hour later. This allowed him to

---

Example: It's OK if Business Time Turns into Social Time

We've been discussing time management, and how entrepreneurs must sometimes forgo social or other recreational time to devote to developing their business. However, this doesn't mean you have to become a hermit, or give up all future trips to the gym. Some successful entrepreneurs get clever, and combine social time with other functions, to minimize the social strain that many founders experience.

Some 3 Day Startup (3DS) alumni in Austin came up with a clever way of combining social and startup efforts. When one of them had an idea they were hoping to flesh out or get feedback on, they would invite startup-minded friends over on the weekends around brunch time. They would prepare breakfast tacos (the most popular brunch item in Austin) and juice, and over brunch, the group would complete a Lean Canvas or complete ideation exercises for the business concept they were exploring. After about an hour and a half, there was a well-evaluated business idea, including plans for future steps. The friends enjoyed this time as well, because they got (1) brunch, (2) a chance to catch up with friends, and (3) an opportunity to explore entrepreneurship ideas, which they thought was enjoyable and interesting.

While this example presents a way to get some productivity out of social time, it does not replace time dedicated solely to working on a business. A serious entrepreneur will still have set aside time for business development, usually at the expense or other leisure activities. However, most founders are so passionate about their business that it becomes a labor of love, and they do not feel as if they are missing out on anything by doing so.

Finally, this is not the only way to combine social time with something else without sacrificing social interactions. Other examples include going to the gym with friends, or having work parties (where friends meet up but work on separate things — it's fairly common among graduate students). Get creative, and you will think of ways to make the most of your limited time.

maintain the benefits of going to the gym, while cutting his time spent there approximately in half.

Planning and time management can go a long way to managing time effectively. While it might seem counter-intuitive (spending time planning that could otherwise be used working), it will help your work time be more directed and productive. Even spending 10–15 minutes planning for the next day can make a significant difference.

10.4 Outsourcing (Contract Work) as a Startup Development Tool

The term outsourcing is most commonly used when referring to multinational companies that have manufacturing and other labor-intensive actions completed in developing countries to take advantage of lower labor and regulatory costs. However, the term can be used to describe any work contracted to a party outside an organization. Many startups successfully use outsourcing for product development, quality control, and scaling to keep up with growth. This outsourcing can be international, but it can apply to local help outside of a startup. This is the type of outsourcing we are referring to in this chapter, and its usefulness for development of business concepts (If you're interested in the other kind, Thomas Friedman's *The World is Flat* does a much better job describing it than we could).

The primary advantage of outsourcing is that it can speed up business development which would otherwise be constrained by your time. This is especially prominent when working at another job or handling other significant responsibilities. Further, it is a way to bring in outside help without obtaining a cofounder or employees. While it can be useful to have a cofounder, bringing someone on board that will own equity in the company, and have major influence in its future direction is a huge commitment, and founders are frequently not ready for this at an early stage of startup development. Further, even with one or multiple cofounders, there will be skills that you currently don't possess, which can be acquired for a short time through outsourcing. As an entrepreneur, you will realize that time is a limited commodity, and you will have to prioritize what actions to undertake, and what can be put off until later.

Outsourcing also allows you to utilize skills you might not currently possess. For example, you might have extensive expertise related to software development, but none for graphic design. You could obtain a copy of Photoshop, and teach yourself how to make the graphics your startup needs. However, you will obtain results much more quickly if you were to outsource work to a graphical designer. Further, the time needed to learn this new skill will come at the expense of other startup-related actions (remember, time is especially constrained when you have a startup and a day job). You will learn new skills as a founder, and outsourcing is in no way a replacement for this. However, it is often faster and more time-efficient to initially find outside expertise to help with some startup-related tasks.

Many founders are hesitant about outsourcing since it does cost money. Like time, funds are also a scarce commodity within a new business, and many founders are hesitant to spend money on a task they believe they can complete themselves. However, this thought process fails to acknowledge that time is a limited resource and conserving it for critical tasks can be highly valuable. Further, by outsourcing a job to a contractor, they can have an expert complete a task much more quickly than they would.

One way to consider the cost/benefit of outsourcing is to assign a monetary value to your time. This can be easy to do if you are paid hourly (or by dividing your annual salary by the number of hours you work per year). Next, estimate the time it would take for you to complete that task, and cost to outsource it to an outside worker. You can calculate the "cost" of a task as (hourly time value) × # of hours required. If this cost is greater than the cost of outsourcing, it might make sense to outsource the task. However, if it is lower, it is likely more cost-effective to complete the task yourself. Some effective entrepreneurs also realize that they can use outsourcing as a time multiplier for their startup development, as elaborated in the following case study.

Turning an Hour of Labor into 90 Minutes of Startup Development:
A Case Study

A 3DS Austin alumni and former head organizer named Sartaj is the founder and CEO of Mayu Studios. This company makes apparel with embedded sensors to be used for making live electronic music. They are developing a novel wearable tech product, which includes design work and development of textiles, sensors and electronics, and software.

Before quitting to work on this venture full time, Sartaj worked full time as a front-end software developer. Knowing he couldn't devote himself fully to Mayu Studios, he outsourced a number of jobs or tasks to independent contractors. He still worked on software development for the product, and spent almost every evening and weekend writing code for the product. He also worked as a manager of all product development, and made sure everyone contributing to product design was in sync and working collaboratively.

In Austin, Sartaj was able to hire seamstresses for $25/hour to work on designs that he made. While expensive, it significantly increased the speed of product design as he did not have the bandwidth to work on software development, sensor design, and textile design all at the same time. These seamstresses were also more skilled at sewing than Sartaj, and were able to work faster than he would on the same task. This allowed him to quickly make and test prototypes, and collect feedback from likely customers more effectively than if he did all the sewing himself.

Increased productivity was not the only benefit to outsourcing though. Beyond his day job, Sartaj was also able to take on consultant work, which typically paid ~$60/hour. Even after taxes and expenses, earnings from a single hour of his consultation work were worth more than an hour of work from a seamstress, leaving him with extra funds to invest in further developing his product. Outsourcing was valuable to Mayu Studios because it allowed Sartaj to leverage an hour of his work into more than an hour of textile development for the product.

(*Continued*)

(Continued)

> This system can be advantageous in many other areas as well. If you lack a particular skillset needed for your fledgling business, this can be a way to fill that gap until finding a cofounder or employee to do so. Many new businesses only need a skillset for a short period of time, and outsourcing is a way to gain this without giving up equity or hiring full time employees. As a result, outsourcing remains a promising way to develop businesses in their early stages.

10.4.1 *When to recruit contract workers vs. employees*

While outsourcing can be a great tool for new businesses, it cannot account for all personnel needs for a startup, or completely replace cofounders and employees. Founders must determine when to pursue contract workers versus full-time employees. There are advantages and disadvantages for each, which can make one or the other a better fit based on the highly variable current needs of the startup.

Outsourcing is advantageous when you need a particular skillset for a limited period of time. For example, if a startup was running a one-time crowdfunding campaign, they might need help from someone with campaign management experience. However, once completed, this crowdfunding expertise is likely not a necessary or prudent cost for the startup to maintain. It is easier to have a labor contract end and not be renewed than to fire a startup employee. Further, contract workers typically do not receive equity in the company. This is advantageous for founders that want to keep as much equity as possible. However, it means that from purely monetary standpoint, outsourcing is typically more expensive than permanent workers are. Outsourcing can be used on an ongoing basis, and many startups do this for some needs (for example, many new businesses manage customer service and payroll this way). This is primarily done when the needs for a particular skill are sporadic, or not enough for a full-time employee at the startup. However, it must be considered on a case-by-case basis, and needs will vary even within individual startups as they continue to evolve.

Alternatively, recruiting permanent workers (including both cofounders and employees) is advantageous in certain situations as well. When there is a skillset that is needed on an ongoing basis, it makes sense to have an employee who can provide this skillset for an ongoing period of time. For example, a startup that is constantly updating their website user interface based on customer feedback will continuously need expertise in UI design. Further, employees/ founders receive equity in a business, usually in exchange for a lower monetary compensation than they might receive at a large company. In addition to being cheaper than contract workers in a solely monetary sense, it also often leads to a greater level of commitment — these people are much more likely to work late nights and during time off than contractors are, because they have a personal stake in the company, and they want their equity to gain value.

For both contract or permanent workers, recruiting is one of the most important decisions a founder can make. It requires significant time and effort, as it can have a significant negative effect if done incorrectly. In a startup, every employee/contract worker represents a significant percentage of manpower. For example, if a company with 200 workers makes one bad hire, that represents 0.5% of the workforce that is not optimal for the company's needs. If a startup with 4 workers does the same, it would mean 25% of all manpower was misaligned. Even though time is a scarce commodity, you should put extensive effort into recruiting personnel for either contract work or as cofounders/employees — the downside of a mistake is too high to make these decisions lightly.

10.5 Conclusion: When Do I Quit My Day Job to Work on My Startup Full Time?

The question above is one that we frequently hear from entrepreneurs wanting to take their startup to the next level. There is no single correct answer to this question — it will vary greatly for each individual founder and startup. It is important to consider a variety of startup and personal circumstances to determine if you are ready to work for a startup full time. The following are some of the questions we recommend you to consider when evaluating taking this plunge.

10.5.1 *Business questions to consider*

Am I confident this business will continue to grow?
No one wants to work on a middling or unprofitable business. While it's ok if your startup isn't that right away, it has to quickly find a way to do so. You should be confident that the business you are working on at least has the potential to grow into a profitable or full-time venture.

You might find that the business is unlikely to be profitable. This occurrence is ok as well. One advantage of not plunging into a startup full time is that it gives you time to get to a go/no go decision while minimizing disruption of other life circumstances.

What is the fume date of the startup? Do I have adequate resources to allow it to succeed?
The term "fume date" refers to the time when a company runs out of money and is no longer able to operate (it is based on the expression "running on fumes", which is when a gas-powered vehicle is out of all fuel except gasoline vapors). If the fume date of your startup is 2 weeks, that is a much more precarious situation than if it is 6 months. Further, joining a startup full time will likely change this date, as working on a venture full-time often consumes more resources.

Even if there is no near fume date, you want to ensure your startup has adequate resources to not constrain development. For example, if the answer to this question is less than 6 months, it might indicate a shortage of resources that could constrain other startup actions.

What surprises or unforeseen changes might occur in the future?
As we stated previously, startups can change rapidly. While it is impossible to predict these perfectly, you can prepare for more likely changes, and how to address how they might affect business development.

As much as possible, you want to anticipate any potential changes, and how it might affect the viability of your startup. Further, will these changes affect the appeal of joining a startup full-time?

10.5.2 *Personal questions to consider*

Am I passionate about this business?
You must be passionate abut your startup, as this will give you the drive to dedicate significant time and effort to growing this business.

When you join a startup full time, there is an opportunity cost of the alternatives you are forgoing to do so. In situations like these, you want to have a lot of faith in your business, and that it is the best opportunity you can pursue to do so.

What happens if the business doesn't succeed? Am I confident that I can find another job easily?
While it is never wanted, many startups do fail, even when founders do everything correctly. In this event, you will have to find another position. Sometimes this is a very quick process — we know 3DS alumni that have received multiple job offers after a week of searching and interviews. Other jobs (like being a professor) are much scarcer, and take longer to come by.

Will my lifestyle be significantly impacted by this change?
Even if you receive a salary/benefits from your startup, it is likely that they will be lower than those you receive from working for a large company. Your current lifestyle expenses might exceed what you earn at a startup. While some people are fine with downsizing to eat ramen and sleep on a futon, others have back pain, and need a memory foam mattress in an apartment without roommates to be comfortable. Other times, people don't want to give up health insurance for their children. Lifestyle situation and needs can vary greatly from person to person, and you must consider how you will be affected by moving to a startup.

Will family or other relationships suffer by doing this?

Working longer hours at a startup can mean forgoing other social time. While good friends and family will be understanding when you pursue something you are passionate about, they will see less of you. If you have extensive family commitments, you should consider how they will be affected by long hours spent working on a startup. Further, if there are any ongoing responsibilities (i.e. taking care of a parent or children), you should plan for how to manage these before moving to your startup full time, so that the transition is as unobtrusive as possible.

The list of questions above is in no way comprehensive for consideration when pursuing a startup full time. Further, no single question (including those not listed above) is more important than others — importance will also vary for each individual and business. Our main recommendation is that you consider both business and personal concerns before making any definitive decision. It is up to you to decide when to take the plunge of going to your startup full time. Once again, you are in the driver seat, and know better than anyone else what decision is best for you and your fledgling venture.

Reference

1. Kim, L. (2016, January 26). Multitasking is Killing Your Brain. *Mission. org*. Retrieved from https://medium.com/the-mission/multitasking-is-killing-your-brain-79104e62e930#.hcmtllmry.

Chapter 11

The Art of the Side Hustle

11.1 Introduction

As we discussed in the Chapter 10, not all businesses are a full-time endeavor. When you see stories about startups, they will often emphasize dramatic actions, like a student dropping out to work on an idea they believe in, or an employee quitting their day job on the first day of starting their new business. However, this is not the only (or even typical) way businesses are created. Frequently, startups start out as something done in addition to a separate full-time position. This can continue for months or even years before the business gains its first full-time employee (which is usually a founder, that works for no or low salary). In addition, some startups will always remain a part-time endeavor and never become the primary employment for its founders.

The phrase "side hustle" is an increasingly common term used to describe a business that is done in addition to another job/endeavor (like being a full-time student). The phrase has many different embodiments, and there is no single universal definition. It sometimes refers to a part-time job that someone has working for another company (i.e. like driving for Uber). Other times, it is used to describe businesses without full-time employees. It sometimes is even used to describe hobbies that have a bit of earning potential (i.e. if your hobby is woodworking, selling some of the pieces that you create). While this term will probably continue to evolve in the future, it can be confusing due to its diverse meanings and applications in the world of startups today.

There are many different kinds of businesses that fall under this umbrella term. Ultimately, this is a good thing, as it shows a recognition of the diversity of entrepreneurship opportunities that one can pursue. Further, by including multiple types of entrepreneurship, it can be more inclusive of individuals from different backgrounds, and is not limited to a few fields that have been historically prominent (like tech). However, this can be challenging to individual entrepreneurs aiming to classify their business venture further.

In this chapter, we will try to briefly outline different kinds of side hustles, and some specific considerations for each type. In Chapter 6, we mentioned that venture funding is not always accurately portrayed in media. The same is true of side hustles, and many do not realize the breadth or scope these businesses can take. Once again, we are not advocating for any one type over another — We are merely trying to lay out various possibilities, so that you can accurately consider which category your business falls into (if any), which can help direct future actions and strategies.

11.2 Types of Side Hustle Businesses

11.2.1 *New/growing startups*

In the last chapter, we discussed how to grow a new business while working "full time" on something else (i.e. school, a job, etc.). This is one of the most common types of side hustle businesses. In Chapter 1, we discussed the reasons that working for a startup appeals to many people, and these reasons also cause them to want to fully immerse themselves in this type of career. As a result, many see a side hustle as a temporary step to their business growing up into a venture they can work for full time.

The ultimate goal of this type of business is to grow until it can support a full-time job for its founders and other employees. As a result, founders with this type of side hustle must always be thinking of ways to grow the business. One of the key focuses is to not let these businesses stagnate, and to continually be identifying opportunities for growth. While founders must manage multiple tasks based on importance, this will remain prominent regardless of startup stage.

However, founders must be aware that not all startups are suitable for this designation. You must be able to realistically evaluate your venture in regards to opportunities for future growth. If growth opportunities are limited, you might need to reconsider how you view these side hustle businesses, and if it falls into one of the other categories mentioned in this chapter. It is not a bad thing if this is the case, but if you are set on working for a startup full time, this might make you consider pursuing a different venture entirely.

11.2.2 *"Always side hustle" businesses*

For some businesses, it can be very difficult/impossible to grow large enough to become one that supports full-time employment. There are multiple possible causes for this: Some businesses will never have enough customers to have full-time employees. Other times, in order for a business to grow, it will need large rounds of investment/capital that the founder does not want to pursue. This is not a bad thing (unless you are very set on developing a full-time venture), and might even appeal to some people who don't want to work for a startup full-time (we have included an example of this situation on the following page). Side hustles can still be a good source of income and entrepreneurial activity, even if they have an overall limit to their size or growth. Further, working on an "always side hustle" business can teach you entrepreneurial skills that can be used in the future on a full-time venture.

Even though these businesses will remain a part-time endeavor, it is still important to treat them like businesses, but on a smaller scale. It is important to emphasize customer validation, and making sure you have enough paying customers to become profitable. Further, the founder of these ventures should be considering ways to scale up business activities to maximize profitability, even if there is an upward ceiling. Finally, you must still carefully consider what is the best use of your limited time, and how to balance the multifaceted responsibilities that come with managing these businesses.

Example: Entomology Themed Jewelry Side Hustle

Kayla is a friend of 3 Day Startup (3DS), and an entomologist that works to preserve wild bee populations throughout the Midwest. In her spare time, she creates and sells insect-themed jewelry based on her work. She sells these products through insect conferences and organizations, and as of this publication is starting to explore online sales channels as a promising opportunity to grow sales of her products.

Even though this is not her primary job, Kayla still treats this venture like she would a full-time business. She utilizes the Lean Canvas to develop her business framework and make small adjustments to improve profitability. Further, she chooses designs and products based on what sells best with customers, not what she enjoys the most. Overall, Kayla spends about as much time on non-creation elements of the business (i.e. marketing, investigating new sales channels, analyzing customer feedback, etc.) as she does on creating new jewelry designs (which can be more fun and enjoyable).

Kayla has accepted that her jewelry business will probably never become her full-time job — there likely aren't enough customers for insect-themed jewelry. Further, she enjoys working as an entomologist, and wouldn't want to give that up. As a result, this business will likely remain a side hustle for the foreseeable future. Still, she enjoys having a small business and a reliable income stream outside of her job. This honest evaluation of her venture allows her to pursue a (part-time) business opportunity that fits well with her personal goals and work situation.

11.2.3 *"Income stream" side hustles*

Some people want a secondary income stream in addition to their full-time job. To do this they might try to work extra hours at their job, or get a second, part-time job. Some will also turn to side hustle businesses to provide this income stream. For founders that pursue this route, making as much money as possible is a high priority, and can even be more important than the business idea itself. As a result, these individuals might gravitate towards business concepts that are lower risk and less innovative. They might also pursue business concepts and frameworks that reach profitability more quickly as well. They also might choose a business model that feels more like a "job" than a startup as well.

Once again, there is nothing wrong with income being the primary motivator for a business — it just means that your priorities are different from others. However, if there are opportunities to make more money elsewhere, you might elect to do this over a side hustle business. Still, income is not the only benefit of these side hustles. You will still gain skills and expand your professional network with these concepts, as you would with other side hustles or full-time startups.

11.2.3.1 *Evaluating the viability of side hustle businesses:*
   The Uber Rule

One way to evaluate the attractiveness of these side hustles is something we call "The Uber Rule." This rule is summed up with the question "Can I make more money driving for Uber/doing another part-time job in the same amount of time?" If the answer to this question is yes, you might want to consider doing something else that will allow you to maximize your income stream.

It is important to note that the Uber Rule is not the only way to assess side hustle businesses, and primarily applies to those where an income stream is a predominant priority. There can be many other reasons to keep working at these businesses, even if the answer is yes. It can be a great way to learn startup skills and build a professional network for future entrepreneurial endeavors. Further, side hustle businesses can sometimes also help with other professional pursuits (for example, working as a tutor helps us improve our teaching skills, which helps our day jobs as professors).

Further, the Uber Rule will vary greatly based on the individual. For example, software developers can often get lucrative hourly gigs writing software. As a result, despite its name, the Uber Rule does not just apply to driving for a rideshare company. Each potential founder must customize the assessment based on what they could earn based on their skillset and local opportunities.

While the Uber Rule can be a good way to assess side hustles, it is not a set truth. Further, it doesn't apply as prominently to other types of side hustles. However, it can still be used as a tool to help inform founders. A good business is always open to adjusting to pursue better business opportunities, and entrepreneurs should be willing to do the same. If profit is a predominant motive of the founder, the Uber Rule can be a good way to assess if a side hustle is the best use of their always-scarce time.

11.3 Passion Projects

There are some businesses that start primarily as a hobby/passion project. This is a dream for many people (getting paid for something you do for fun). While some people can make a full-time career of their hobby, these jobs are rare and extremely competitive to obtain — for example, the number of people that want to be YouTube personalities/content creators on a full-time basis is multiple orders of magnitude greater than the number of people that actually are able to do so. As a result, many people try to monetize their hobby in some form as a side hustle in addition to their regular job.

While it is true that a hobby can generate revenue, this is not always the case. Some hobbies (i.e. woodworking or jewelry making) are easier to monetize than others (i.e. entertainment). Further, there are many others that try to monetize their hobby as well, and the competition you will face is almost always higher than average for other businesses.

The mindset of the founder can also be different for this type of side hustle. You might choose to focus primarily on creation/the most enjoyable aspects of the project, and as a result will not be actively working to maximize profitability. Further, the object that these founders create might be based on personal interest rather than customer demand. This is what distinguishes these passion projects from Always Side Hustle businesses — they do not prioritize actions based on customer needs and growth. There is nothing wrong with pursuing passion projects if you gain enjoyment or fulfillment from a hobby or recreational activity. Further, it is not mandatory that you try to monetize your hobbies. However, it is important to consider these endeavors differently than other types of businesses. These are far less likely to return a profit, or grow into a larger or full-time business, and you should not count on them doing so.

Another thing to consider is that if you try to monetize a hobby too much, it might destroy your interest in said hobby. As soon as you attempt to monetize a hobby, you must shift some of your focus to what creates value for customers instead of what you actually enjoy doing. If you enjoy creating value or solving problems for customers, this might not lower your enjoyment from this shift. However, for some people, the financial return might not outweigh the loss of enjoyment in said activity. You do not need to attempt to monetize every aspect of your life, and time dedicated to hobbies can remain separate from entrepreneurial actions.

For example, consider cooking as a hobby vs. running a restaurant. Cooking for fun entails discovering new flavors, and creating items that you personally enjoy eating, regardless of time and effort required to do so. Managing a successful restaurant entails many additional tasks, including (but not limited to) managing inventory to avoid spoilage, making food customers will buy, and keeping costs (including labor) low enough to retain profitability. In fact, cooking and creating new flavors is a very minor percent of time entailed in running a restaurant. Subsequently, there is often a case to be made for looking elsewhere for potential side hustle or full-time business ventures.

11.4 Conclusion

Entrepreneurship is much more complex and diverse than how it is often portrayed in media and pop culture. There is no single image or type of business that is indicative of all startups — they can be highly variable in terms of industry, growth strategy, and more. Scale of business (i.e. side hustle vs. full time) is yet another way entrepreneurship can be highly individualized. Many founders create side hustle businesses, and while some of them grow into full-time ventures, many remain this way for years or in perpetuity. As a result, founders must be aware of side hustle businesses, and factor them into consideration when forming their entrepreneurial goals.

Even within a specific type of businesses like side hustles, there are various embodiments that you can pursue. While each embodiment can become a successful business, some might be more suitable than others based on a founder's goals. In order to determine this suitability, you must be able to accurately and honestly evaluate your business concept. Even if this assessment produces discouraging findings (i.e. the type of business you are creating does not match your personal entrepreneurial goals), it is important to be honest when evaluating your business concept. Throughout this book, we have stressed the importance of being honest, even if it produces negative findings. Remember, founders and their business concepts change rapidly, and you can always pivot to improve your business to make it more aligned with your preferences.

Index

Printed in the United States
by Baker & Taylor Publisher Services